I0419520

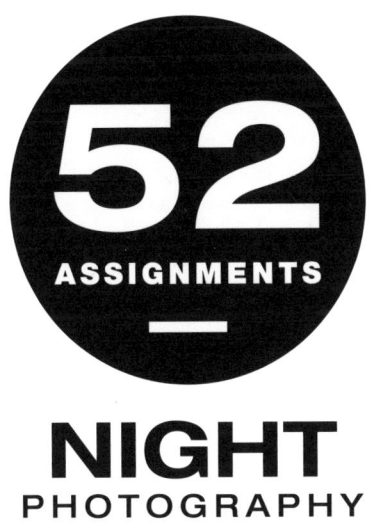

NIGHT
PHOTOGRAPHY

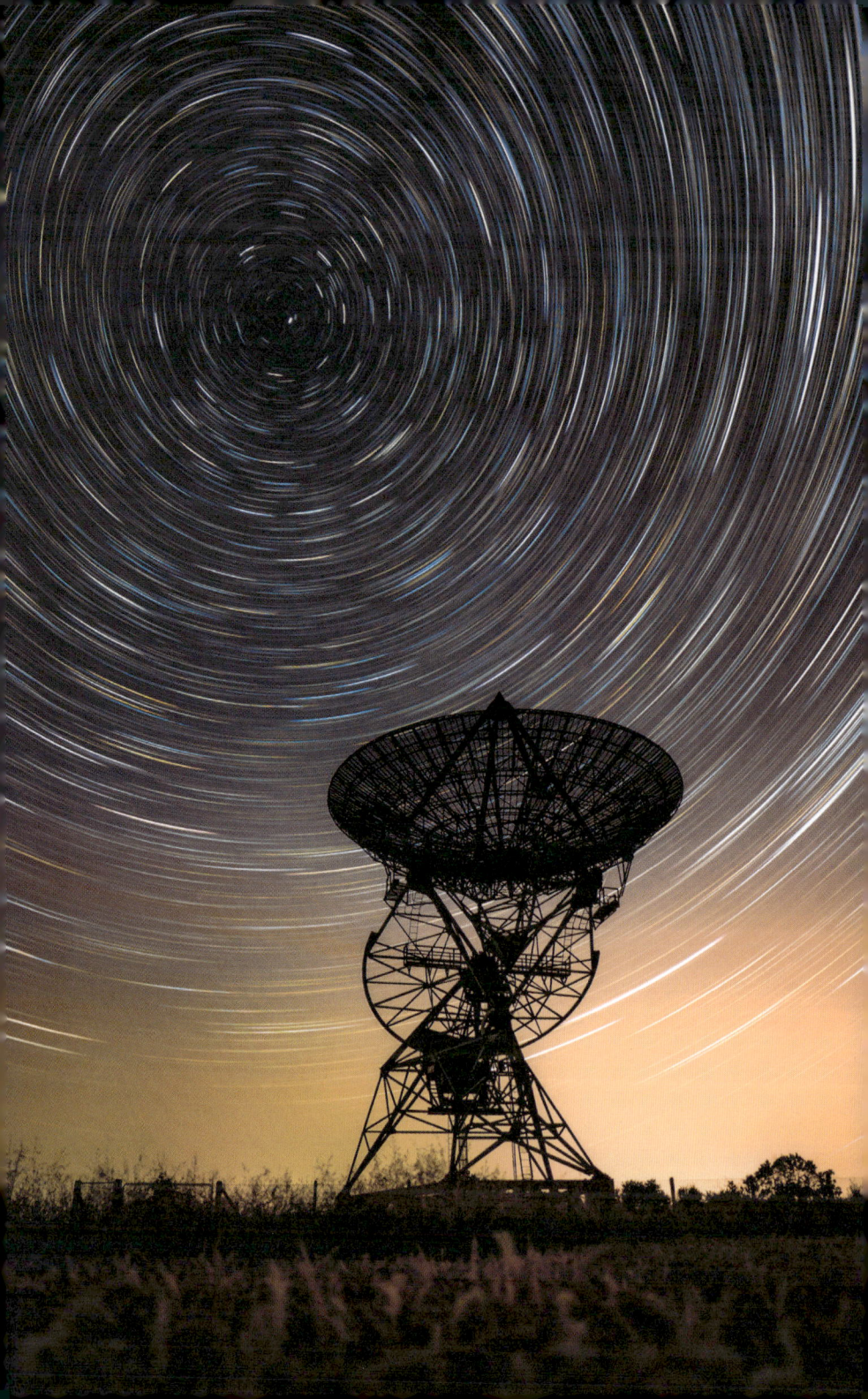

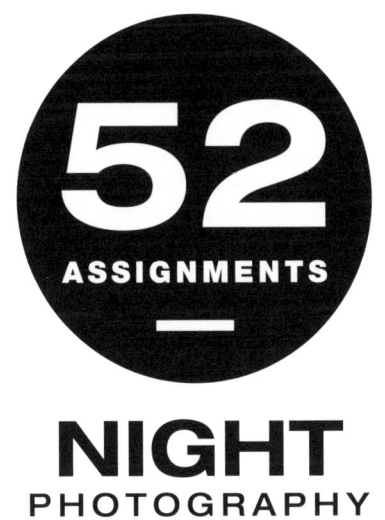

NIGHT
PHOTOGRAPHY

JOSH DURY

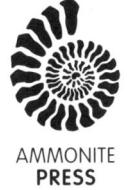

AMMONITE
PRESS

ASSIGNMENTS

Tick off your completed projects

ASSIGNMENT KEY

Each assignment has symbols showing the type of tasks involved.

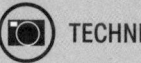 TECHNIQUE

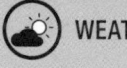 WEATHER

 RED FLASHLIGHT

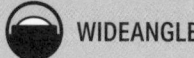 WIDEANGLE

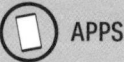 APPS

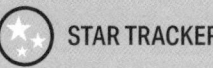 STAR TRACKER

EQUIPMENT

 JOURNAL

 LOCATION

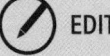 EDIT

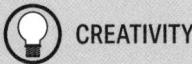 CREATIVITY

 RESEARCH

INTRODUCTION

The night sky is truly magical. From comets to meteor showers, auroras to eclipses, these celestial wonders remind us of the immensity of our universe. Night photography acts as a bridge between art, science and culture, with advances in cutting-edge technology helping us to be more attuned with the night sky than ever before. However, with light pollution and the ever-increasing number of artificial satellites, our view of the night sky is changing before our eyes. This is why I firmly belief we need to be passionate about our natural environment in order to protect it.

These 52 assignments will show you how to photograph these natural wonders. They will help you to plan your shoots, master the various camera techniques, and build your confidence as a night photographer. You don't necessarily need the latest or most expensive equipment—I will help you to optimize your existing setup to take the best images possible.

Night photography is very different from "day" photography. Perhaps the most obvious difference is that you are shrouded in darkness and—assuming you are photographing in a dark-sky area—the only light sources are the stars shining above you. Another key difference is exposure—in the dark, long shutter speeds, wide apertures, and high ISOs are settings you become accustomed to.

In terms of accessories, there are three essentials: a red flashlight, a durable, lightweight tripod, and a remote shutter release. Red flashlights emit a red light to help you see in the dark while preserving your night vision. A tripod and remote shutter release will keep your camera steady and minimize camera shake during long exposures.

Since I was seven years old, I've been mesmerized by the night sky, and I would like to thank my family and friends and my supporters from around the world who have made my journey to the stars as a professional astrophotographer a reality. I hope this book and the assignments inspire you to look up at the beauty of the cosmos.

Josh Dury
B.A. FRAS.

NIGHT PHOTOGRAPHY BASICS

From camera settings and techniques to accessories and fieldcraft, there's a lot to think about when shooting creative images at night. Here is a quick overview to get you started.

CAMERA SETTINGS

Mode: For creative night photography, switch your camera to Manual mode ("M") to take full control of camera settings, then adjust and balance the shutter speed, aperture, and ISO to achieve the desired exposure. These settings work together to increase the signal-to-noise ratio (SNR) of our images. I'll discuss key considerations in each assignment.

Shutter speed: Night photography and long exposures go hand in hand. Whereas on a bright day, a typical shutter speed will be a fraction of a second, in the dark exposure times will be seconds, minutes, or hours depending on what you are photographing. However, pinpoint stars will start to become trails of light beyond exposure times of 30 seconds due to Earth's rotation, so as a rule of thumb, keep your shutter speed below this level unless instructed otherwise.

Aperture: Your camera's aperture works in the same way as a human eye. In bright light, pupils constrict to limit the amount of light that enters the eye. In dim light, pupils dilate to allow more light into the eye. So, for night photography, we need to use the widest aperture possible. For many lenses, this will be f/2.8, but some lenses go as wide as f/1.8 and even f/1.4. The wider the aperture, the more light that enters your camera.

ISO: This setting determines how sensitive your camera's sensor is to light and how clean or noisy your final images appear. The higher the ISO, the more obvious the noise, so approach with caution—set ISO to 640 as a starting point and work your way up. If in doubt, use your camera's rear LCD monitor and zoom function to take a closer look at image details and assess your current camera settings.

White balance: It's best to use custom white balance settings rather than relying on your camera's Auto White Balance. I recommend a white balance setting between 4,500-5,500 Kelvin (K) for replicating a natural white balance. You can always "correct" white balance in post-production.

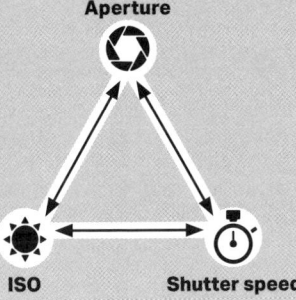

Aperture

ISO   **Shutter speed**

◄ *Shutter speed, ISO, and aperture can be thought of as three interconnected settings which can be adjusted to produce a properly exposed photograph.*

SIGNAL-TO-NOISE RATIO

Digital noise is similar to analog film grain and is an undesirable consequence of using high ISOs. The signal-to-noise ratio (SNR) is a measurement used to compare signal to noise for a digital camera sensor. A high SNR means that image detail clearly stands out from the background noise, while a low SNR means image detail is harder to distinguish from the noise. As light pollution is the most significant source of noise in night photography, the simplest way to achieve a higher SNR is to shoot away from towns and cities and/or use a natural-night filter.

FOCUSING

Focusing in the dark can be challenging. Your camera's autofocus system is effectively rendered obsolete due to the lack of light and so we must focus manually to achieve pin-sharp images. Often, temporarily illuminating your foreground subject with a flashlight and selecting your camera's widest aperture will provide enough light for you to focus via your camera's rear LCD monitor—zoom into your focal point to obtain focus. When focusing on stars, again use your camera's rear LCD monitor and zoom function to focus, slowly turning the focusing ring until the stars render as sharp pinpoints of light in the night sky.

COMPOSITION

Unless you have a super-wide lens that gathers a lot of light, composing in the dark can be challenging. This is why some night photographers opt to arrive on location before sunset, compose their image, and wait for the light to fade. Of course, this isn't always practical, so the alternative is to use your flashlight to illuminate important foreground details to aid composition. Just be careful not to interfere with other photographers' images.

ACCESSORIES

Red flashlight: This is arguably the most important accessory in a night photographer's camera bag. It can take the human eye 30 minutes or so to fully adapt to the dark, at which point white light from a standard flashlight or smartphone should be avoided. Red flashlights help you see in the dark without affecting your night vision and are available as either hand or head flashlights.

Remote shutter release: Camera movement during long exposures will result in camera shake, which is why a remote shutter release is another wise investment. These accessories connect to your camera either wirelessly or via a cable and allow you to trigger the shutter without physically touching your camera. More advanced remote shutter releases also allow you to set a delay after pressing the shutter button, set the number of images required, and set the interval between frames.

Star tracker: A star tracker is essentially an electronic motor that mounts to the top of your tripod and moves at the same rate as Earth's rotation, allowing photographers to shoot long exposures of the night sky without stars appearing as trails of light. They are specialist pieces of kit, but as your skills and confidence improve, you may want to invest in more advanced equipment and a star tracker should be top of your list.

Tripod: A strong, sturdy tripod is recommended for night photography. My preference is for carbon fiber models, as they are compact and lightweight, and their ergonomic design is well-suited to colder environments.

Geared head: An integral part of any outdoor tripod setup, geared heads are mechanical systems that attach to the top of your tripod legs and allow for very precise adjustments both horizontally and vertically—perfect for fine-tuning your compositions.

Filters: The two most popular filters for night photography are diffuse and natural-night filters. Diffuse filters are designed to make stars appear bigger and brighter (see Assignment 16), while natural-night filters reduce the effects of light pollution (see Assignment 36). Neither are essential, but if you are looking to capture a number of visual effects, these are great filters to consider.

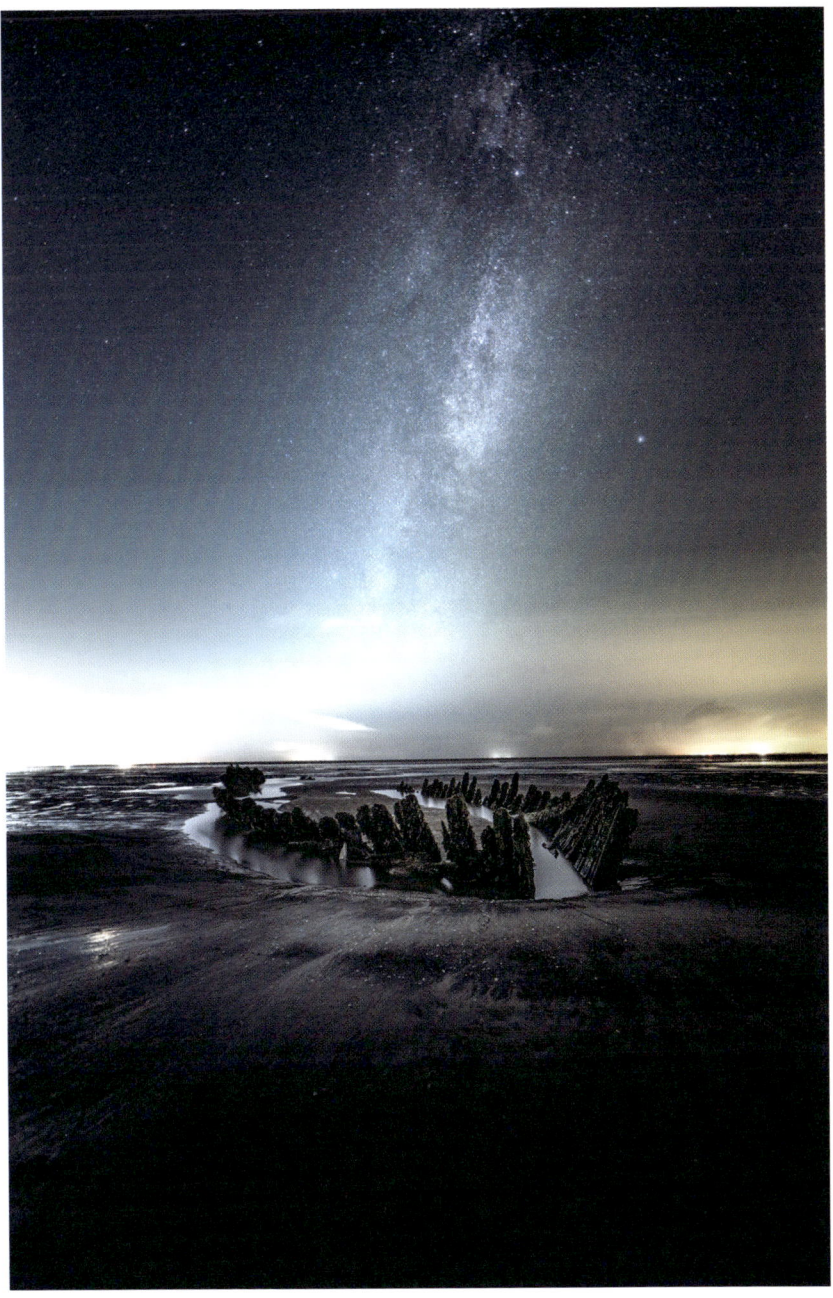

▲ *The shipwreck of the 19th-century sailing ship* Nornen *with the Milky Way shining in the skies above.*

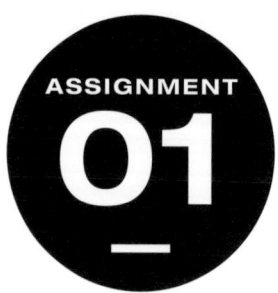

ASSIGNMENT
01

TIPS

- The movement of star trails will become more apparent if using focal lengths of 50mm or more. To counteract this, use shorter shutter speeds.

- Dial back your aperture if the stars aren't clearly visible.

TIME TRAVEL

The light from distant stars travels at around 62 miles (100km) per second. While this movement is imperceptible to the naked eye, it's possible to capture this light through creative use of shutter speed.

Stars can be photographed from your own backyard and are a great subject to practice your night photography skills on. Shutter speeds of 1–3 sec. will capture bright stars as defined points of light, while exposures exceeding 10 sec. will also capture fainter stars. Shutter speeds of 30 sec. and beyond will capture star trails as Earth rotates.

For this assignment, shoot a series of six images of stars, with shutter speeds ranging from 1–30 sec., and see how clearly each exposure renders the subject. Which effect do you prefer? Keep your lens's aperture as wide as possible and select a low ISO between 200–400.

FIELD NOTES

The longer the shutter speed, the more light we let in and the greater the risk of overexposure. To avoid losing important image detail, check your histogram and make sure the peak is off-center to the left.

Underexposed

Overexposed

Correct exposure

◀ *Not letting enough light into your camera will result in an image that is too dark, while letting too much light in will result in an image that is too bright.*

ASSIGNMENT
02

TIPS

- Wide apertures aren't the only cause of vignetting—lenses with longer barrels and filters can block light toward the edges of the frame.

- If using narrower apertures to reduce vignetting, limit your shutter speeds to no more than 30 sec. to avoid star trails.

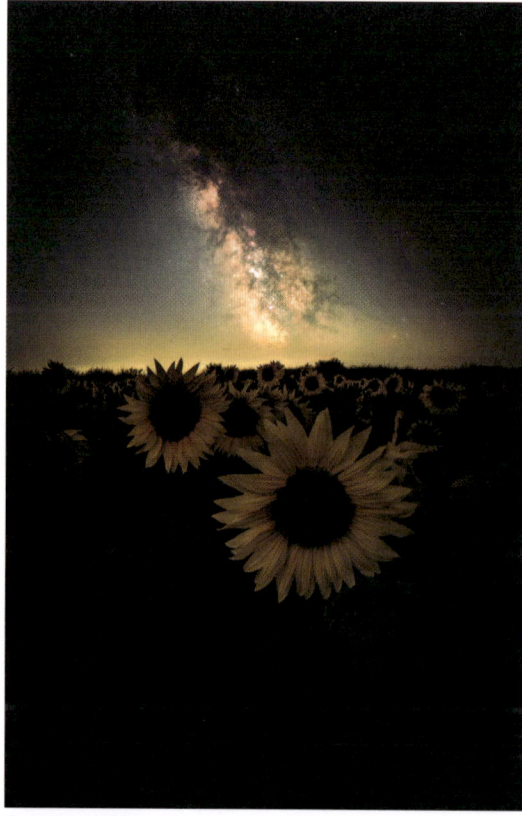

Aperture: f/1.4

CAPTURE THE LIGHT

When photographing celestial structures such as galaxies and nebulae, the general rule of thumb is to let as much light into your camera as possible. However, the use of wide apertures causes vignetting—a gradual darkening of the corners and edges of the frame—which reduces brightness and saturation.

This exercise is designed to illustrate the correlation between aperture and vignetting. Point your camera at the Milky Way (see Assignment 13), set your shutter speed to 8 sec. and ISO to 640, and shoot five images at f/1.4, f/2, f/2.8, f/8, and f/16. Which image has the most obvious vignette? Which image has no vignette at all?

Vignetting can be reduced or "corrected" in post-production. In Adobe Lightroom or Camera Raw, select the Lens Correction module, check Enable Profile Correction, and use the sliders to manually correct the vignetting in your images.

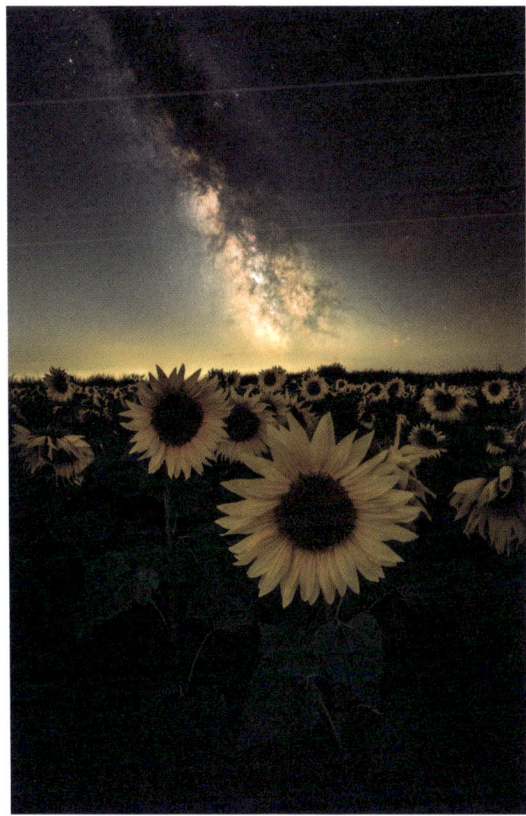

◀ These images demonstrate the effects of vignetting at different apertures. This effect can be used to draw the viewer's eye into the scene.

Aperture: f/2

ASSIGNMENT
03
___

TIPS

- When increasing your ISO, consider adjusting your aperture instead to let more light in and preserve image details.

- Areas with light pollution will require lower ISOs, whereas dark-sky sites will require higher ISOs to capture greater detail.

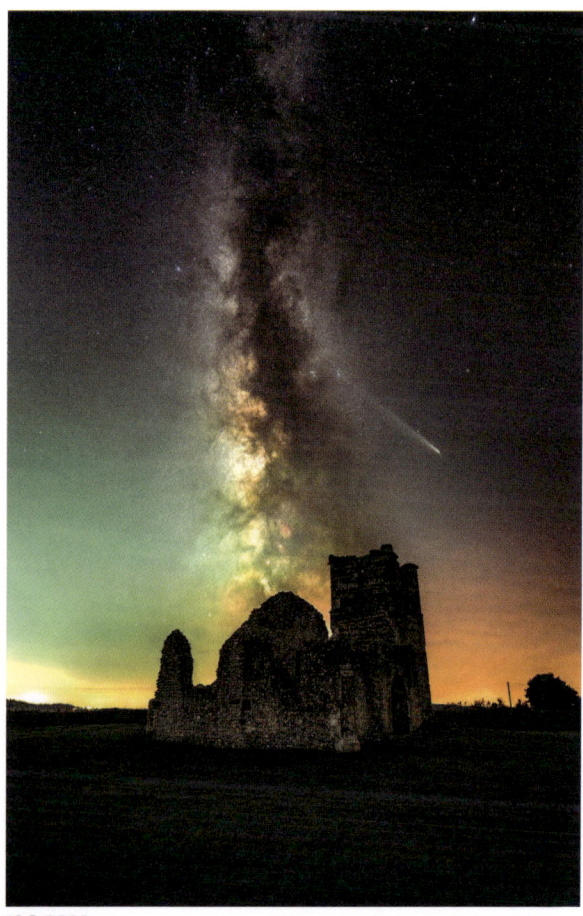

ISO 3200

SIGNALS OF LIGHT

If you want to brighten an image without using a longer shutter speed or wider aperture, you will need to increase the ISO setting. However, this increase comes at a cost—every time you push ISO higher, you degrade image quality by introducing more digital noise. Night photographers get around this problem by "stacking" several exposures in specialist post-processing software, but if you're starting out, it's important to understand the effects that ISO can have on a single exposure.

For this assignment, find a local landmark or body of water, frame your scene with the camera in portrait orientation, and shoot a series of six frames at night using the following ISO values: 100, 200, 400, 800, 1600, and 3200. Make sure that shutter speed and aperture are constant throughout. Then zoom in and compare the results and see which ISO value provides the most balanced exposure.

At the lowest ISO settings, your images will probably be too dark, but as you increase the ISO to 800, light in the foreground and background will be amplified and details will emerge. At the highest ISO settings, a sandpaper-like texture (digital noise) will become visible across the frame and fine details will begin to lose clarity.

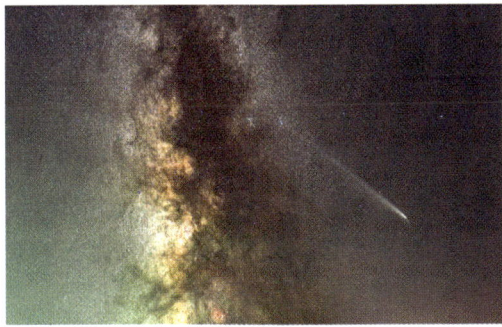

ISO 6400

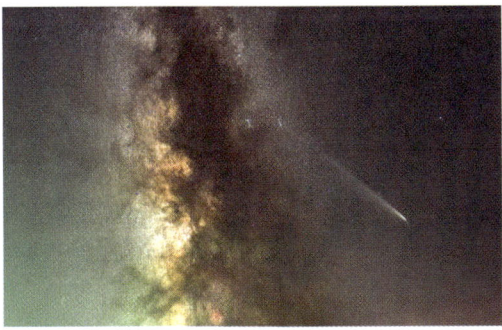

ISO 1600

◄ *Images taken at various ISOs show different levels of detail. This is why it is so important to find the perfect ISO setting to produce the most balanced exposure.*

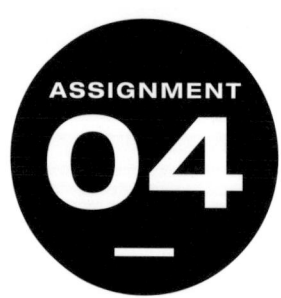

ASSIGNMENT
04

TIPS

- The moon is easier to locate at night due to its relative surface brightness. If using a telephoto, zoom in to your lens's longest focal length and use features on the lunar surface to achieve focus. Search for visible craters or focus on the edge of the moon (the "lunar limb").

- Most digital cameras feature built-in zoom functions that allow you to magnify the image displayed on the rear LCD screen. Use this function to aid manual focusing.

THE CHANGING MOON

Our view of the moon is constantly changing. This is because the lunar cycle repeats every month (29.5 days to be precise) and transitions through eight phases: new moon, waxing crescent, first quarter, waxing gibbous, full moon, waning gibbous, last quarter, and waning crescent. These phases present compelling photographic opportunities, from detailed telephoto shots to wider landscapes.

Your mission is to photograph the changing moon in a creative way, choosing the style and technique you think is most appropriate. For close-up images, use a telephoto lens. For landscapes that feature the moon, use a wider lens. If photographing during the day, use your lens's widest aperture and an ISO of between 100 and 200 (shutter speeds will be much faster than when shooting at night). Take a series of exposures and see which ones capture the most amount of detail.

FIELD NOTES

The moon rises approximately 50 minutes later each day. As a result, moonrise and moonset times change constantly. There are numerous astronomy websites and apps that predict these times, although www.timeanddate.com is arguably the most reliable. Set your geographic location and plan your assignment accordingly.

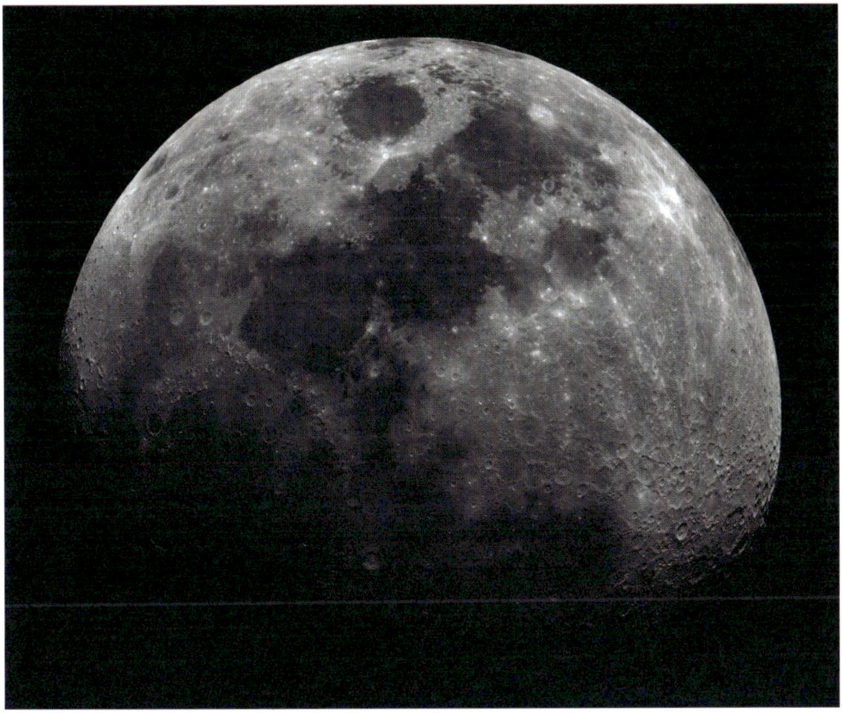

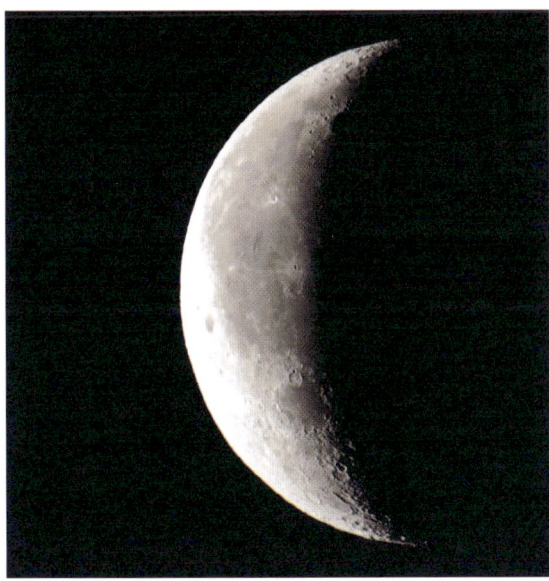

▲ ◄ *Photographing the moon on subsequent nights will reveal its changing phases. Look along the "lunar terminator"—the line that divides the light and dark sides of the moon—to see which craters and other features are visible.*

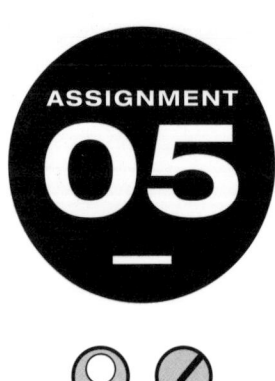

ASSIGNMENT
05

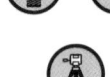

TIPS

- Locating the moon is easier if you deliberately overexpose by a few stops. Don't forget to correct your exposure before triggering the shutter, otherwise your images will be overexposed.

- To capture as much detail as possible, select a low ISO value and experiment with settings until you find your camera's "sweet spot" for a balanced exposure.

REGOLITH MOON

The moon is a fascinating subject to observe and photograph. With its numerous phases, craters, and "faces," it has mesmerized astronomers for centuries. To the naked eye, our only permanent natural satellite appears rather monochromatic, but did you know that it's possible to reveal the "colors" of the moon? For this assignment, you will be enhancing the saturation of the moon to reveal its array of "regolith" (the term used to describe the layer of loose material found on the moon's surface), the color of which varies depending on its composition.

You will need a telephoto lens with a minimum focal length of 400mm or even a small telescope (special accessories called T-rings and T-adapters will allow you to attach your camera to a telescope). A sturdy tripod and a remote shutter release are also essential to minimize camera movement as much as possible.

To locate the moon through your camera's viewfinder, start at your lens's shortest focal length and zoom in, keeping the moon in the center of the frame. Focus manually using your camera's LCD screen and magnification function, zooming in on the lunar limb (the edge of the moon's visible surface) or a crater for an area of clear contrast. Select your lens's widest aperture, set ISO to 160, and adjust shutter speed to balance your exposure.

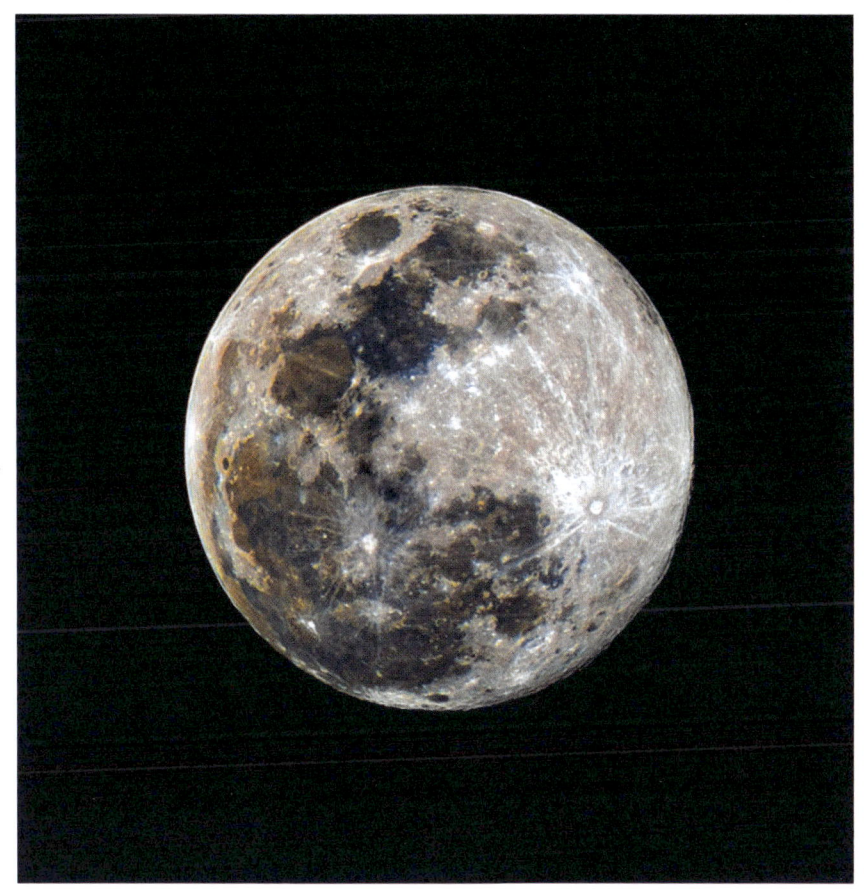

▲ *You know you have a strong image that captures the moon's natural colors if there is a fine balance of yellow and blue hues (but don't oversaturate these details). You will be left with an image that tells the story of the moon's geology.*

When viewing your unprocessed images in photo-editing software, the moon will appear monochromatic, but by gently increasing the Vibrance and Saturation levels, the moon's previously unseen yellow and blue hues will start to appear. How far you increase these adjustments is a question of personal preference.

ASSIGNMENT
06

TIPS

- Keep the moon in the center of the frame to minimize distortion and allow for a clear blend in post-production.

- If using a star tracker, adjust your speed to "lunar tracking" once polar aligned.

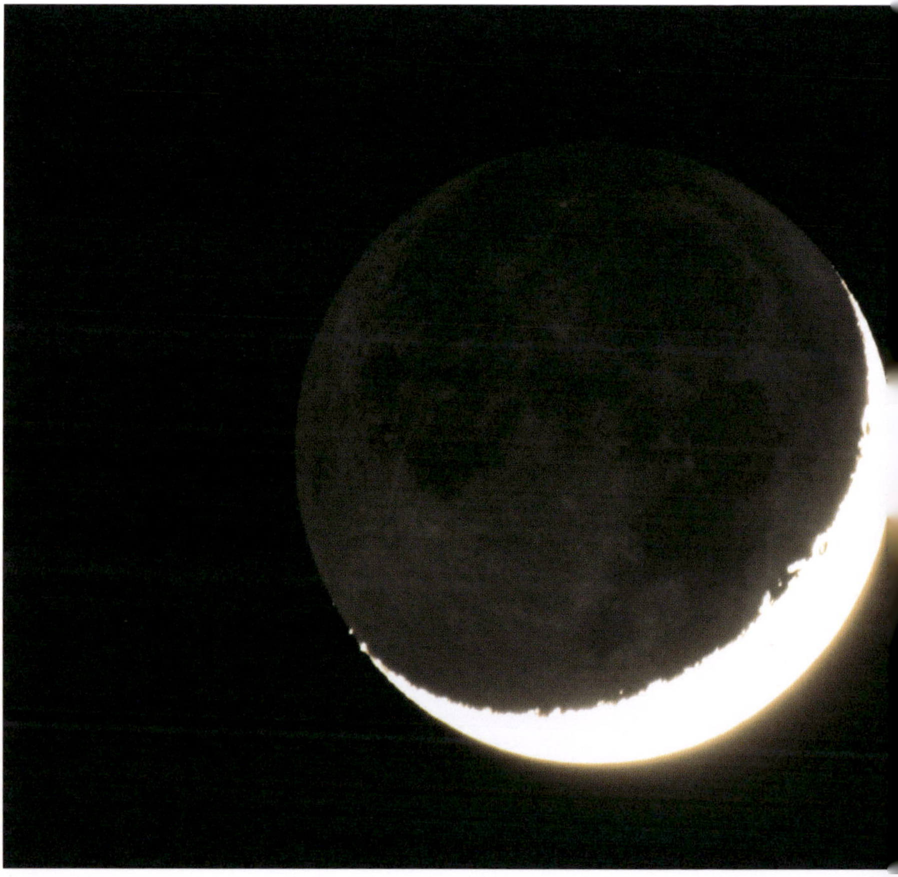

EARTHSHINE

If you've ever looked at a crescent moon and noticed a diffuse glow around the darker areas of the lunar disc, you've witnessed a phenomenon known as "earthshine." This occurs when light from the sun reflects off the surface of Earth. This effect is best captured around either the waxing crescent at dusk or the waning crescent before dawn.

The line that divides the light and dark sides of the moon is called the "lunar terminator." Craters and lunar seas along this line will be partially lit, making for some dramatic lunar imagery.

Your assignment is to capture and create an image of earthshine, using a telephoto lens to fill the frame with the moon. Select your camera's lowest ISO value to preserve as much detail as possible.

◄ *Earthshine was captured in this image by using a long exposure, which reduced the details visible on the moon's surface.*

FIELD NOTES

Exposing for the details on the surface of the moon is challenging due to the extremes of the dynamic range. To get around this, we can shoot and blend two exposures—one for the lit side of the moon and another for the unlit side—using the high dynamic range (HDR) technique discussed in Assignment 10.

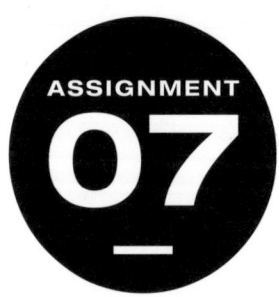

ASSIGNMENT

07

TIPS

- A focal length of 400mm or more is preferable but not always necessary, as it depends on your creative intent. Planetary details will require such extreme focal lengths, while lenses with a wider field of view will capture planetary objects as pinpoints of light.

- A star tracker is advised for this assignment, as the more accurate your polar alignment, the more detailed the results. See Assignment 29.

OCCULTATIONS

The term "occultation" refers to any event in which one object is hidden behind another passing object. In astronomy, this occurs when the moon passes in front of a star, planet, or other astronomical object. Lunar occultations are relatively frequent, occurring a few times each year, and are fascinating events to observe and photograph. Your assignment is to capture the exact moments a planet disappears and reemerges from behind the moon.

As the moon is significantly closer to Earth than other celestial objects, your visibility of a lunar occultation will depend on your exact geographical location, so planning and research are vital. An excellent resource is www.lunar-occultations.com, which lists all forthcoming "bright star" occultation events around the world. It even includes free downloadable software that allows you to generate predictions for your area and view fainter occultations. In terms of weather, clear skies are preferred, as lunar occultations can last for several hours.

While the technique for capturing lunar occultations is the same as photographing the moon (see Assignment 4), the trick here is to capture your individual frames at intervals of around 60 seconds. In post-processing, align and blend these "sub" images into a single frame.

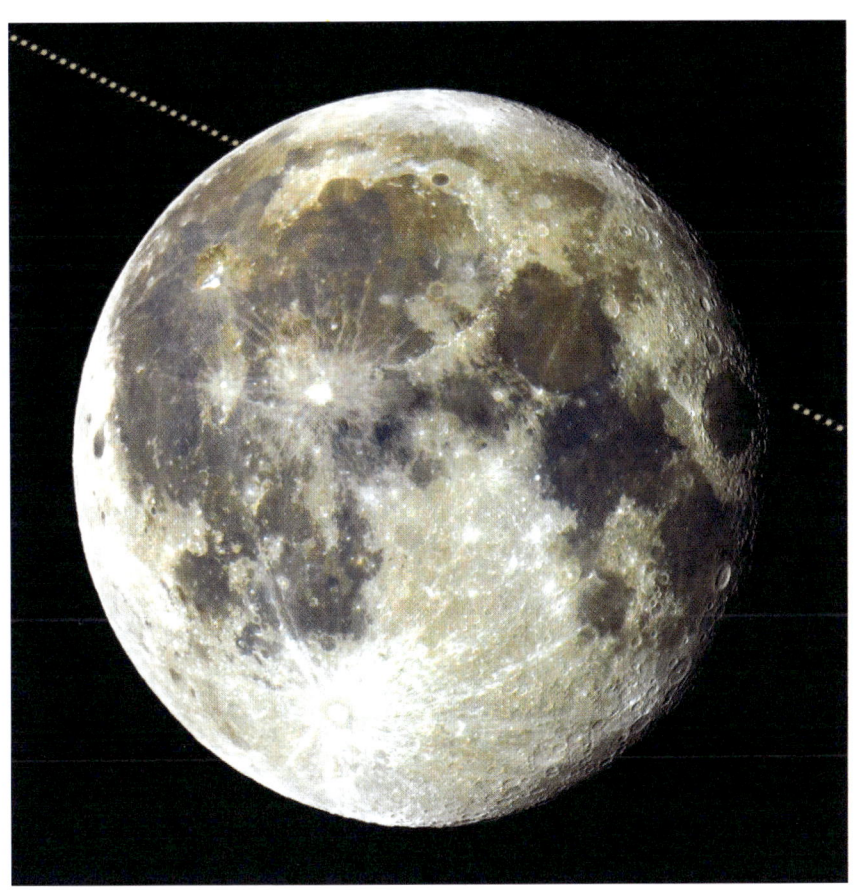

▲ *I merged 30 images into a single frame to create this image of Saturn hiding behind the moon as it passed in front.*

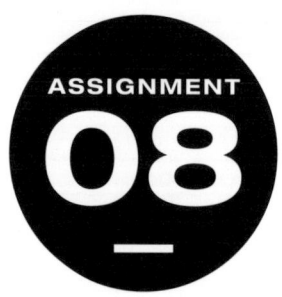

ASSIGNMENT
08

TIPS

- When capturing these style of images, the ISS can be lit or unlit depending on its orbit around the Earth. During an unlit pass, pay close attention to timings in order to capture the transit. Lit passes are often easier to capture as the ISS can be observed approaching the moon.

- Keep checking your focus before the transit, as atmospheric turbulence can affect the sharpness of your images.

▶ *The International Space Station as it appears to graze the surface of the moon. This is a composite of images captured over a duration of just 1 second.*

TRANSITS

Whereas lunar occultations occur when celestial bodies "hide" behind the moon, transits occur when objects appear to pass across the face of a larger celestial body. From Earth, the only planets that pass between us and the sun are Mercury and Venus, and these are rare events, but there is another object that passes between us and the moon that can be photographed far more readily—the International Space Station (ISS).

To find an upcoming transit, visit www.skyandtelescope.org and use the website's Satellite Tracker to refine your search by country, city, or latitude and longitude. The site will then list relevant dates alongside a map of the night sky showing times, duration, and elevation.

To fill the frame with your lunar transit, use the longest telephoto lens in your kit bag, and mount your camera/lens combo to a sturdy tripod. Keep the moon in the center of the frame and trigger your remote shutter release when the transit commences. The ISS travels across the night sky at 17,500mph (28,000km/h), so set your camera to Continuous Drive mode and shoot as many images as possible. Blend them into a single layer at the editing stage.

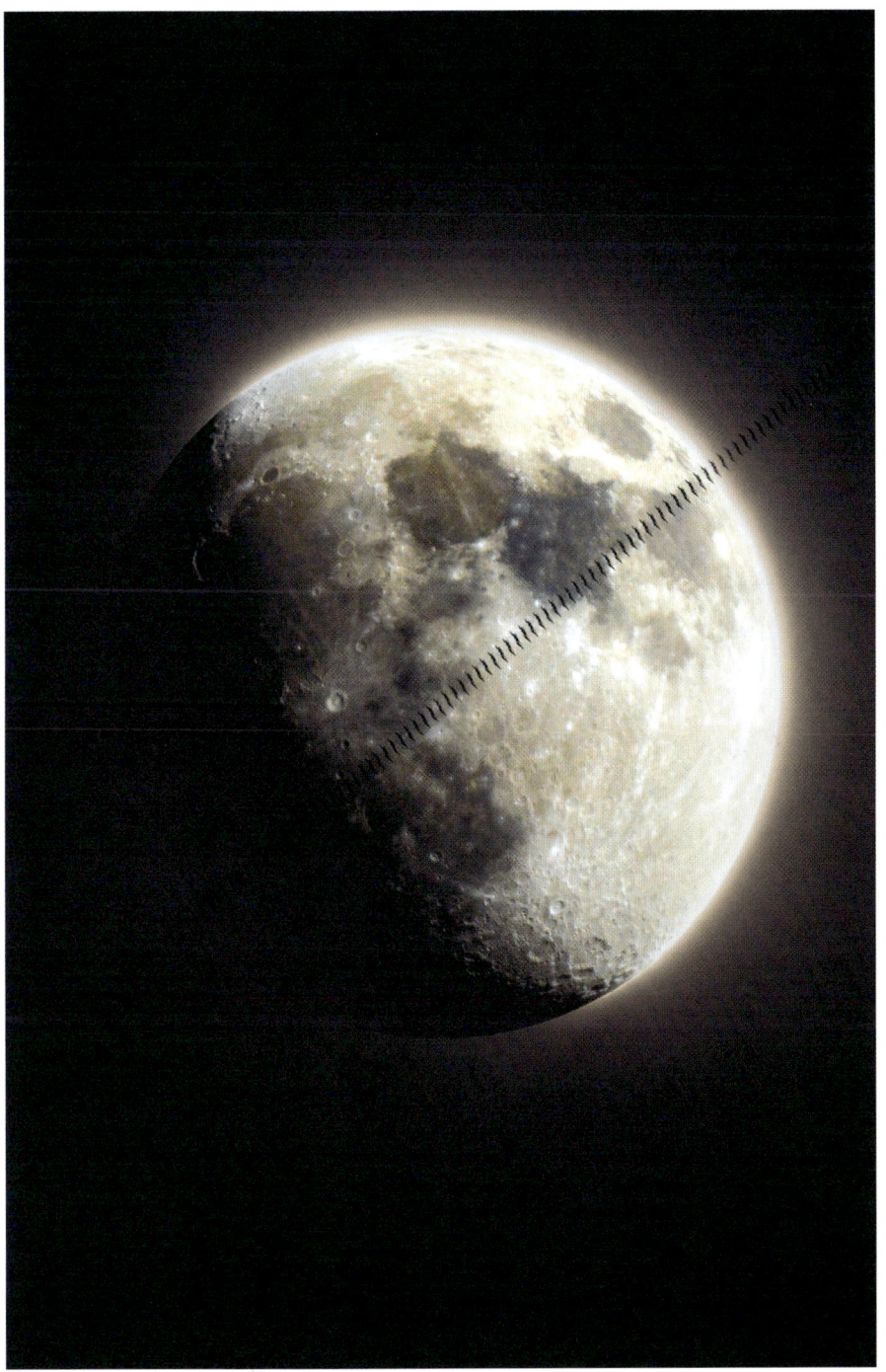

TIPS

- The moon measures half an astronomical degree (roughly the width of your little finger). Use this figure in relation to the information provided by your planning apps to predict the relative height of the moon from your location.

- Keep checking your weather apps, as forecasts are subject to change.

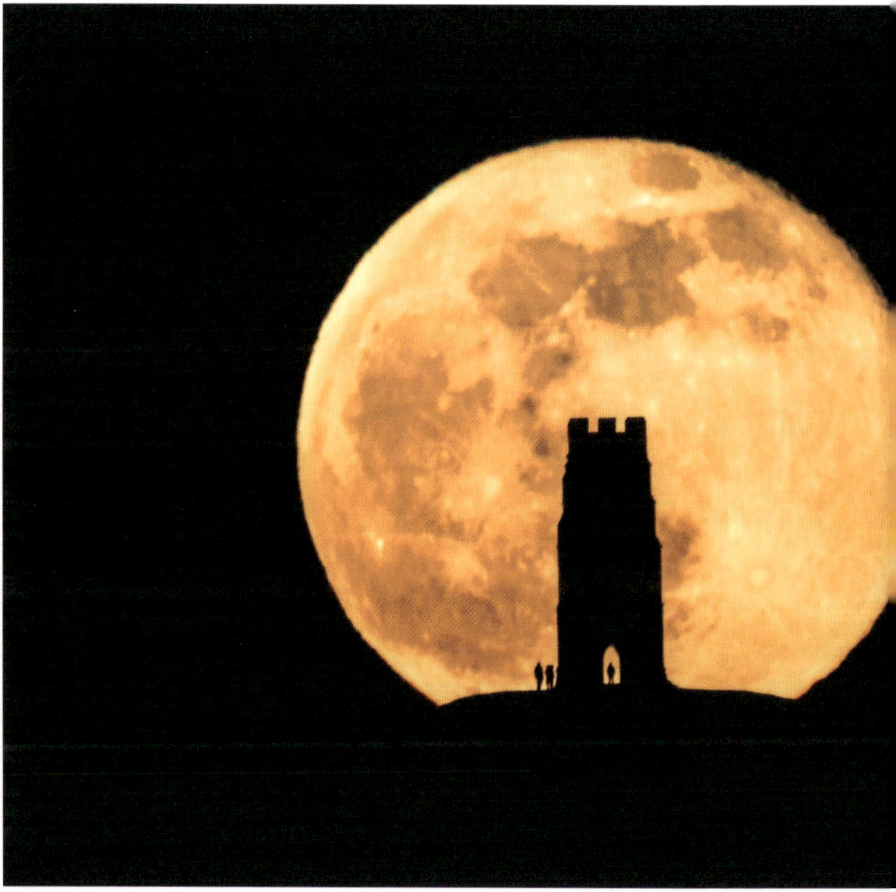

LUNAR ALIGNMENTS

Lunar alignments capture the moon as it appears to rise behind a subject of interest and can yield some impressive images. Subjects that are low to the horizon such as trees and towers can make for interesting focal points. Lunar alignment photography is possible (weather permitting) during any visible moon phase, but for dramatic effect, take your images on or around the time of a full moon.

Establish these critical dates using a lunar calendar app such as My Moon Phase, then choose a suitable location to shoot from. The Photographer's Ephemeris (TPE) and PhotoPills both use markers to create imaginary lines that tell you where you need to stand based on how far away and at what altitude your subject is. Use Google Maps' Street View feature to familiarize yourself with your chosen location and choose a suitable viewpoint. Just remember that not all mapping data will be up to date, so it's always worth a recce of the site before the day of the shoot.

Clouds can obstruct our view of the moon, so use your apps to search for a night with clear skies. Even in less-than-perfect conditions, it's always worth taking a chance in case the skies clear, if only for a short period.

A full moon rises around sunset, so there will be a certain amount of ambient light in your images. Use the longest lens you have to fill the frame with the moon as much as possible—upward of 400mm is ideal—and set ISO to between 160 and 200. Exposure times will vary between 1/400 sec. and 1/1000 sec.

◀ *The full moon rising behind Glastonbury Tor. This image was acquired from about 3 miles (5km) away with a 1200mm lens.*

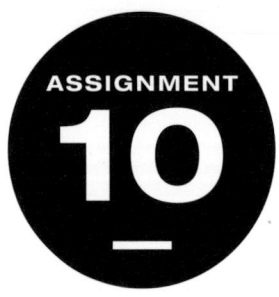

ASSIGNMENT

10

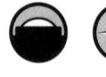

TIP

- While perspective will change when using a wideangle lens, the guidelines for lunar alignment photography still apply—see Assignment 9.

LUNAR LANDSCAPES

The surface of the moon is littered with lumps and bumps as the result of ancient lava flows and meteor bombardment. These are the dark patches we can see with the naked eye. By capturing a lunar alignment (see Assignment 9) with a wider lens, you can include these details to create unique lunar landscapes.

As the dynamic range—the difference between the darkest and brightest parts of an image—will be extreme, the challenge is to balance the exposure across the frame and capture as much detail as possible. To achieve this, shoot three exposures in quick succession, one metered for the highlights, one for the midtones, and one for the shadows, and blend them together at the editing stage. This is a technique called high dynamic range (HDR) photography.

As with the previous assignment, use apps such as The Photographer's Ephemeris and PhotoPills to plan the moon's rising or setting point. On location, consider the size of the moon in relation to the landscape, as this will dictate the scale of your image. Starting at 35mm, increase your focal length depending on the foreground subject matter. Select a wide aperture, set ISO to between 320 and 500, and keep exposures short—1/2sec. to 1 sec. is ideal. Use the camera's histogram to make sure you are capturing as much detail as possible.

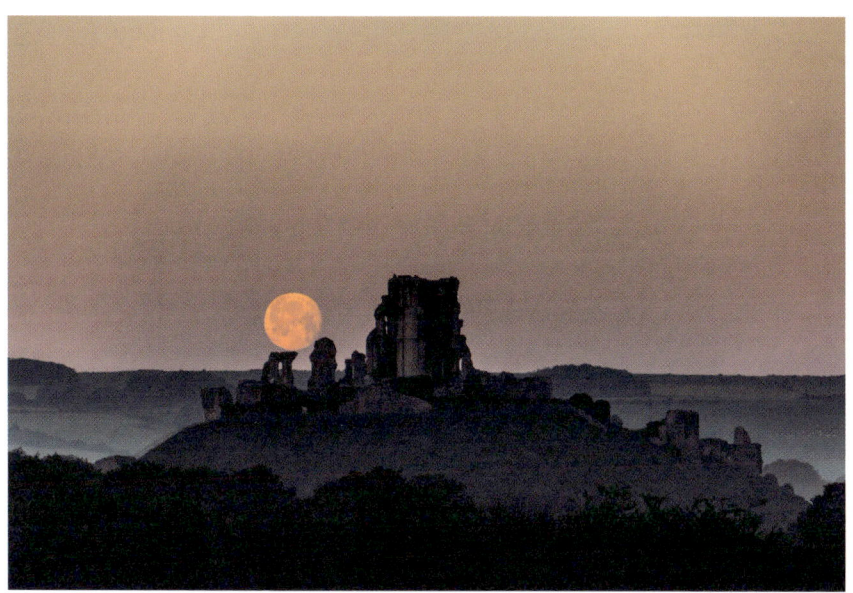

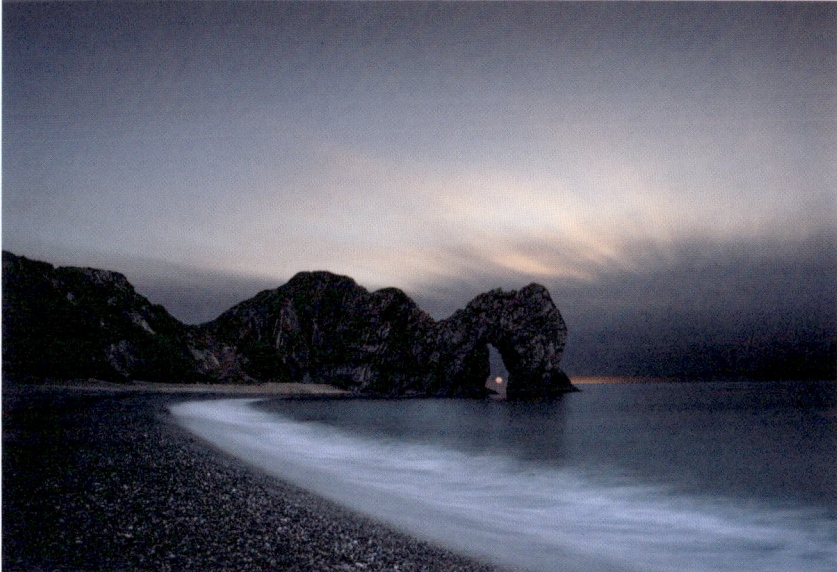

▲ ▲ *The moon appears to balance on top of the ruins of Corfe Castle on a misty morning.*

▲ *A full moon captured as it rises through the arch of Durdle Door. I was shooting alongside two other photographers, both of whom bailed due to poor weather, but I persevered and was rewarded with a short window of clear sky.*

ASSIGNMENT

11

TIPS

- Shorter shutter speeds are best for creating contrast between single light sources and the sky. This is where mirrorless cameras that perform well at high ISOs come into their own.

- Stellarium is a free open-source "planetarium" that shows the sky as you would see it with the naked eye, binoculars, or telescope. Use it to find out which planets will be visible and when. Alternatively, use the Stellarium Mobile app.

THE PLANETS

The planets of our solar system were the first objects I viewed through a telescope as a youngster, inspiring my lifelong interest in astronomy. Not only are the brighter planets—Mercury, Venus, Mars, Jupiter, and Saturn—visible to the naked eye, but under a dark sky, it is possible to photograph the more distant planets Uranus and Neptune.

When two or more planets appear to be close together in the sky from our perspective here on Earth, we observe what is known as a "planetary conjunction."

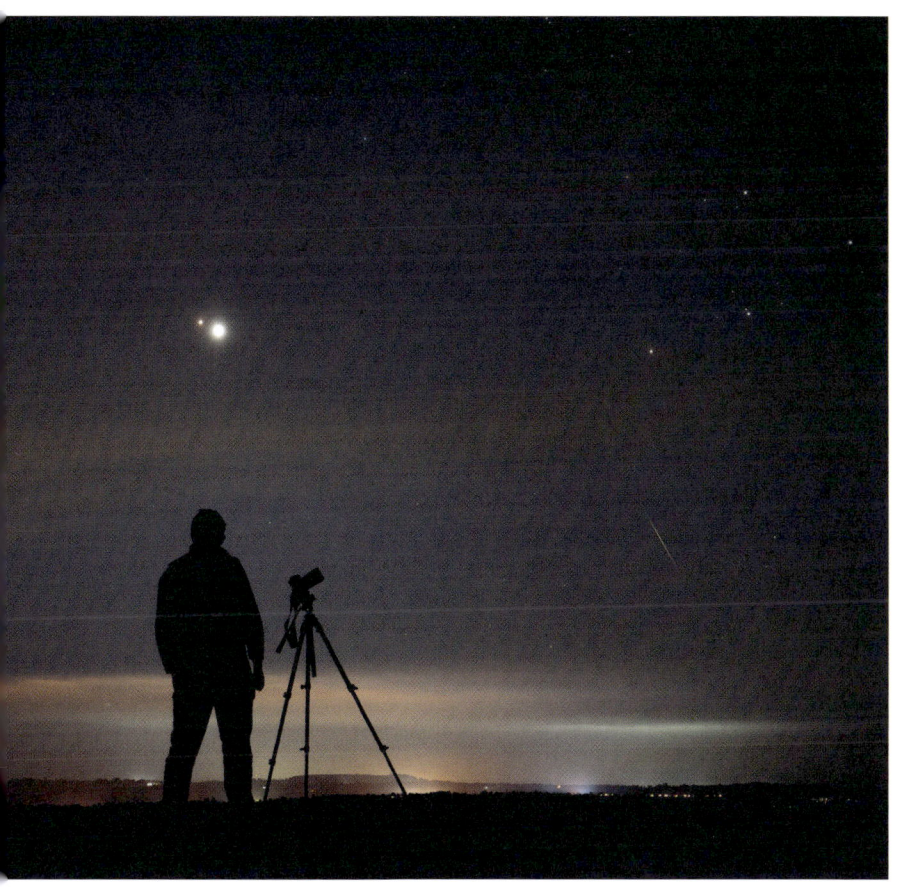

▲ *In August 2024, Mars and Jupiter appeared close together. I was able to capture a self-portrait with this rare conjunction from a high peak.*

These planets are still millions of miles apart, but are fascinating to observe nonetheless. Your assignment is to photograph a "nightscape" of the planets using a wideangle lens.

A wideangle lens around 20mm is all you need to capture planetary conjunctions. You will be capturing singular points of light, so shoot relatively short exposures of between 5 sec. and 15 sec. Keep your lens's aperture wide and your ISO to between 200 and 400.

TIPS

- A wideangle lens with a focal length of around 20mm is a great starting point for capturing planetary parades.

- Look for high, stratospheric cloud, as this can naturally spread light out over a greater surface area and emphasize the appearance of the planets in your images.

- Focus your attention on Mercury, Venus, Mars, Jupiter, Saturn, Uranus, and Neptune. Pluto isn't technically a planet (it's classed as a dwarf planet) and is only visible through a telescope.

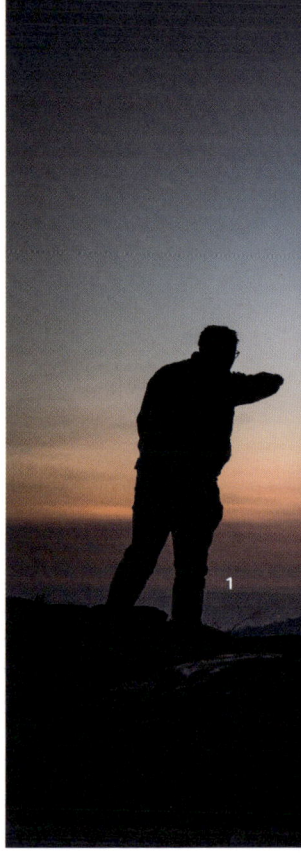

PLANETARY PARADES

Celestial events known as "planetary parades" occur when three or more of our solar system's planets are visible in the night sky at the same time. There will never be a time when all eight planets gather closely, but it's fairly common for up to six planets to align. For this assignment, you're going to be capturing your own planetary parade.

The key to success here is knowing when, where, and which planets will appear to line up, so use a month-by-month guide such as *Philip's Stargazing* to study the planets' movements. We also need to consider the planets' apparent brightness,

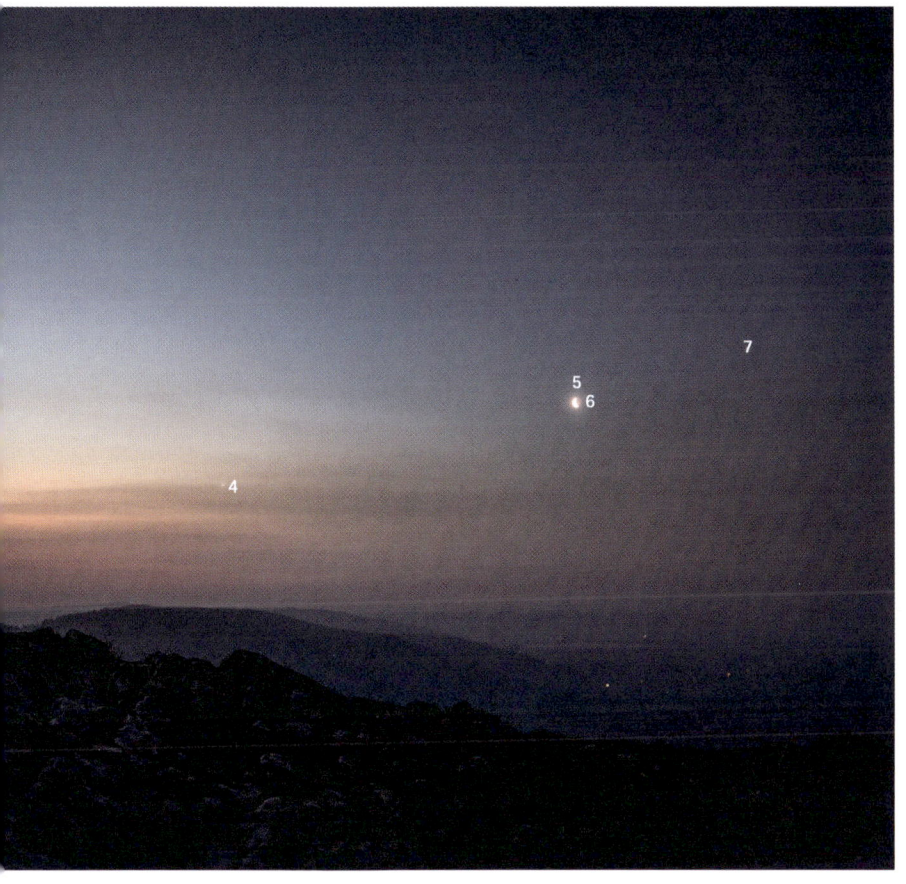

▲ *This annotated image captures the moment when six planets in our solar system and the moon were visible just before dawn. From left to right: Jupiter (1), Mercury (2), Uranus (3), Mars (4), Neptune (5), the moon (6), and Saturn (7).*

which is measured using a "magnitude" scale. The lower the magnitude, the brighter the planet is. For instance, the brightest planet in our solar system is Venus, which has a magnitude of -4.6.

Use your camera's histogram to assess and adjust exposure settings. You want to capture as much image data as possible, so aim for a full histogram "mountain" that peaks to the left—any further to the right and you run the risk of overexposing and losing detail. The planets will appear as single points of light, so start with a shutter speed of 2 sec. together with a wide aperture and an ISO of around 200.

ASSIGNMENT

13

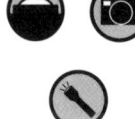

TIPS

- In the Northern Hemisphere, the galactic core is visible from March to October, while in the Southern Hemisphere, it is visible from February to October. The core becomes visible for longer as the months go by, peaking in June and July. Visibility decreases later in the year.

- Astronomy and photography apps such as Stellarium and PhotoPills generate renditions of the night sky to help you plan your compositions.

▶ *The Milky Way's "galactic core" above a poppy field. I composed using the rule of thirds (see Assignment 42) to draw the viewer's eye across the poppies to the Milky Way beyond.*

MILKY WAY

During the warm summer months, when you look up on a clear evening, you might see a faint glow stretching across the night sky. This is the Milky Way, our home galaxy. It is possible to capture spectacular images of the Milky Way with conventional DSLRs and mirrorless cameras—you just need a fast wideangle lens, a sturdy tripod, and minimal light pollution (see Assignment 37).

The center of the Milky Way is known as the "galactic core" and features interesting structural details such as dust lanes (darker, denser material blocking light from the heart of our home galaxy) and bright-emission nebulae (clouds of dust and glowing hydrogen gas). Your mission here is to fill the frame with these structural details. This assignment can be attempted at any time of year, most notably during "Milky Way season," which occurs from late spring to early fall.

In the Northern Hemisphere, the galactic core passes closer to the horizon, whereas from the equator and in the Southern Hemisphere, it appears higher in the sky. This means that longer exposures of up to 10 sec. are required to reveal the core's subtle details and so a star tracker is recommended for this assignment.

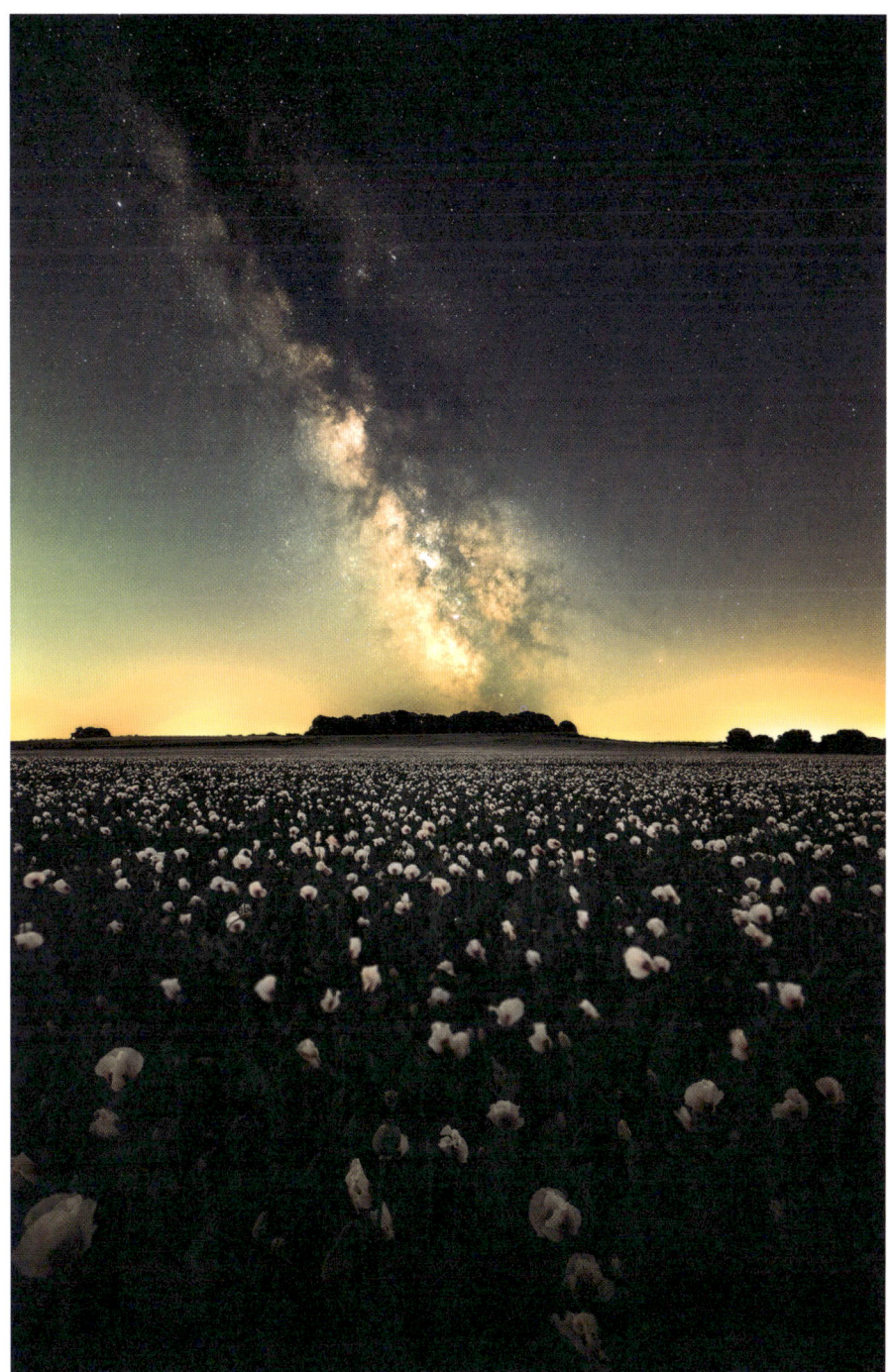

ASSIGNMENT
14
—

TIPS

- The shorter the exposure, the greater the contrast between the night sky and the stars, so aim to keep shutter speed below 5 sec., your aperture as wide as your lens allows, and a low ISO to retain image detail.

- You may wish to consider a diffuse filter (see Assignment 16). These are glass filters used to emphasize the brightness of stars over a greater surface area to distinguish the constellations in your images.

▶ *The "circumpolar" constellations Ursa Major and Ursa Minor, also known as the Great Bear and the Little Bear or Little Dipper, photographed above a picturesque watermill.*

THE CONSTELLATIONS

Constellations are recognizable patterns of visible stars in the night sky. Different cultures around the world have created their own constellations since prehistory, including the ancient Greeks, who used the stars to represent mythological characters and stories. Photographing famous constellations will not only help you get better acquainted with the night sky, but it will also enhance your understanding of the meanings behind the constellations.

Constellations in the direction of the North Star, or Polaris, are referred to as "circumpolar" constellations. They never rise or set but their position in the night sky changes as the year progresses. Other constellations are only visible at certain times of year, according to Earth's orbit around the sun. Once you know which constellations will be visible and where, you can plan your shoots accordingly using photography planning apps such as PhotoPills and Planit Pro together with astronomy apps such as Star Walk and Stellarium.

As a starting point, try photographing some of the major constellations such as Ursa Major, Ursa Minor, and Orion. They make for compelling subject matter through the associated tales of Greek mythology. Can they be used to tell stories in a new light?

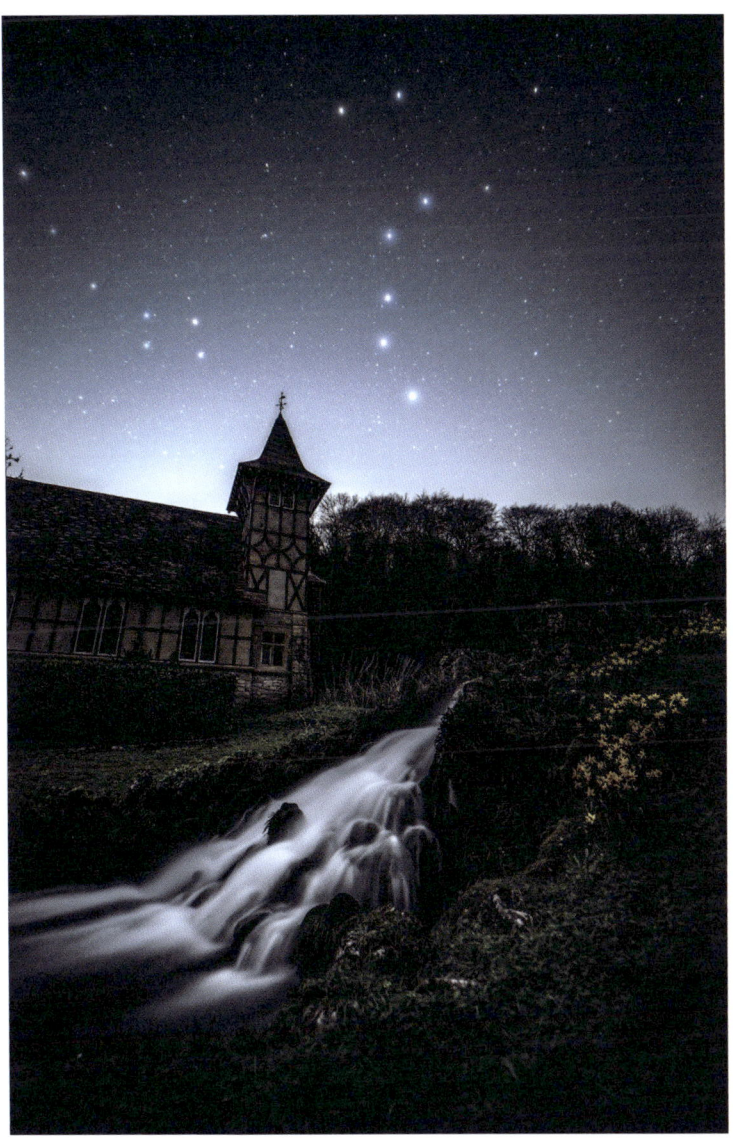

FIELD NOTES

Philip's Planisphere is an excellent reference book that features a movable map of the stars and constellations. It's easy to use, making it ideal for beginners.

STARLIGHT

Most stars appear as single points of white light in the night sky, while a few have orange or reddish hues. This is because as a star's temperature increases, its color changes from red, through orange and yellow, to white and blue. There are various creative techniques you can use to capture these fascinating colors, and for this assignment you will be taking an image of an out-of-focus star to capture light over a greater surface area.

Your first task is to locate a bright star—the brighter the star, the more dramatic the image. Below are suggestions for both the Northern and Southern Hemispheres:

NORTHERN HEMISPHERE
Arcturus: the brightest star in the constellation of Boötes, with an apparent visual magnitude of −0.05. **Vega:** the brightest star in the constellation of Lyra, with an apparent visual magnitude of 0.03.

SOUTHERN HEMISPHERE
Canopus: the brightest star in the constellation of Carina, with an apparent visual magnitude of -0.74. **Sirius:** the brightest star in the constellation Canis Major, with an apparent visual magnitude of −1.46. Can also be seen in the Northern Hemisphere.

Use a month-by-month star guide or astronomy app to locate the star. When a clear night is forecast, use a telephoto lens of 200mm or more to center the star in the frame. Defocus by slowly turning your lens's manual-focusing ring until the star is just out of focus. Push your ISO to 400 to compensate for the longer focal length and start with a shutter speed of 2 sec.

TIPS

- Geared tripod heads allow for more accurate adjustments to composition. Try to avoid accidental movements of your setup, as small movements can make a big difference when using longer focal lengths.

- As you become familiar with this assignment, aim to use higher ISOs and shorter exposures to capture the rainbows of color that emanate from starlight.

▶ *Displayed as a montage, the light from Sirius passes through Earth's atmosphere to reveal a rainbow of color.*

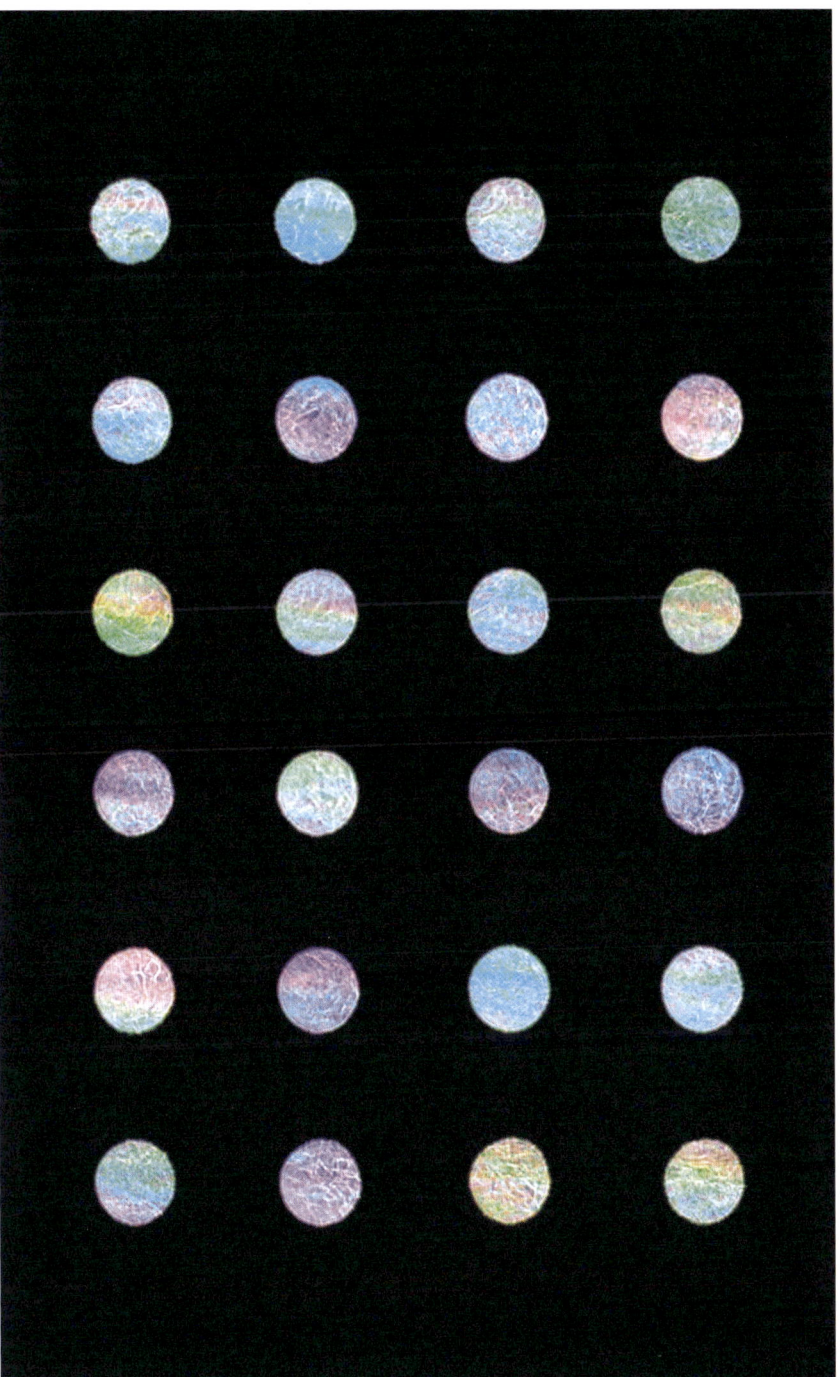

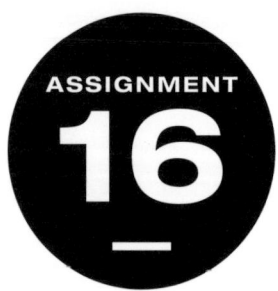

ASSIGNMENT
16

TIPS

• Diffusion filters such as the NiSi Star Soft and the Kase Star Glow are available in a range of sizes. If you can't get the right size filter or an adapter, simply hold the filter close to your lens to prevent reflections.

• Position your filter so that only the sky is covered by the active star-enhancing coating. However, if you wish to be artistic, push the filter all the way down.

▶ *A diffusion filter can be used to capture light over a greater surface area of the stars and constellations, as demonstrated in this scene of the Orion constellation visible over Glastonbury Tor.*

STAR GLOW

When taking images at night, it is possible to enhance brighter stars and constellations with the use of a diffusion filter. These specialist filters feature a textured surface that spreads light over a greater area and work in a similar way to graduated neutral-density filters, with the effect at its strongest at the top of the filter and the bottom third featuring no effect at all. This allows the filters to enhance the stars without affecting your foreground.

For this assignment, take two images of the night sky with a diffusion filter to demonstrate its effectiveness. Start by shooting the constellations (see Assignment 14). Do you notice how the results become more defined? Point your camera at the Milky Way. Do you notice how those brighter stars create further depth in your image?

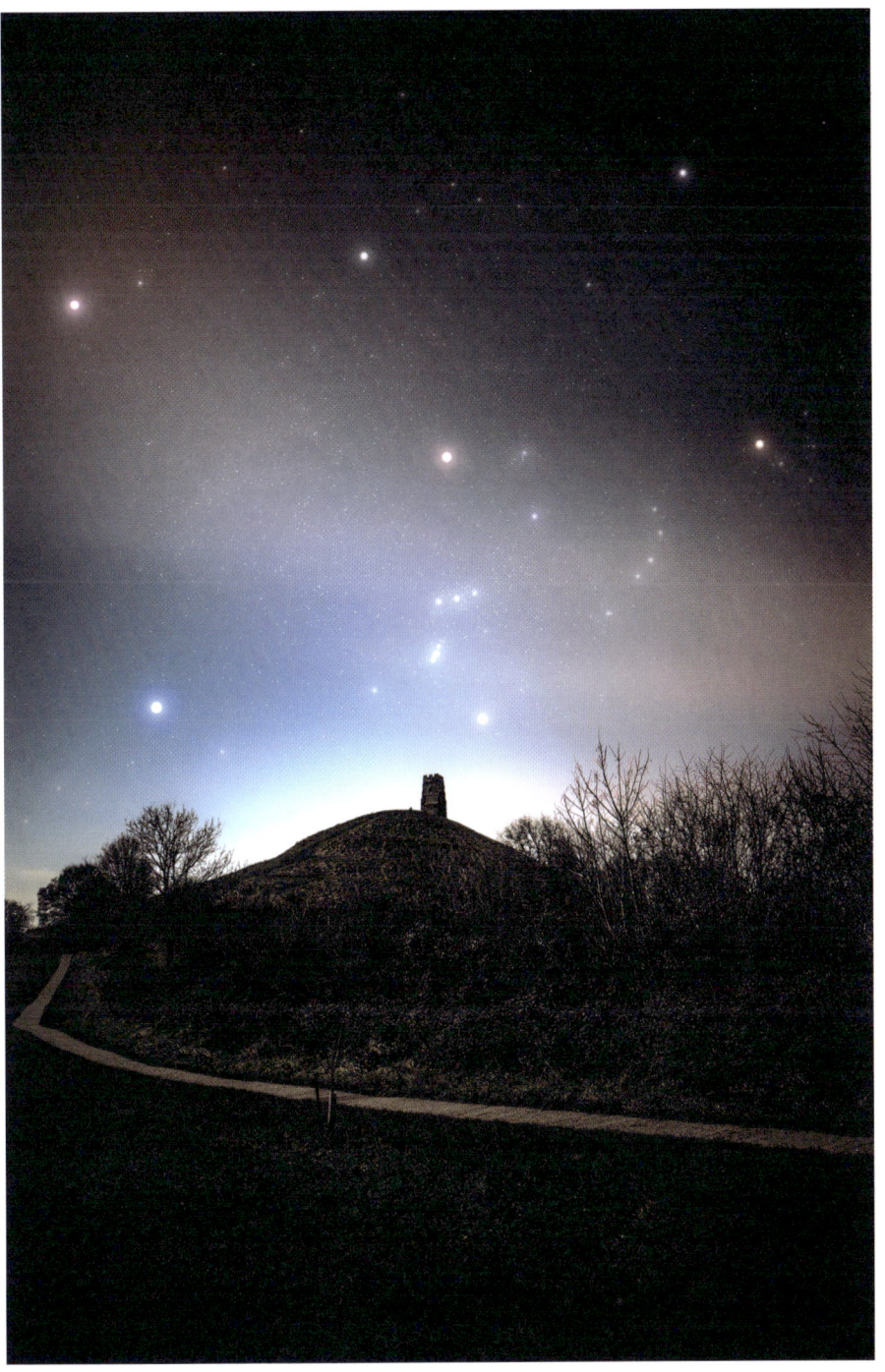

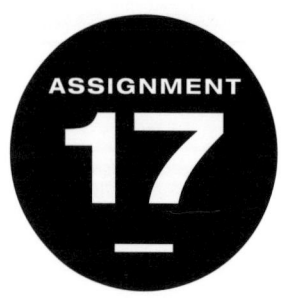

ASSIGNMENT
17

TIPS

- I recommend using a memory card with at least 64GB of storage. Back up any existing images and format your memory card before your star-trail session.

- Carry at least one fully charged spare battery and keep them in a warm pocket to maintain battery life (batteries don't perform as well in cold temperatures).

▶ *I have photographed star trails above Avebury's stone circles numerous times over the years. On this occasion, I shot multiple 8 sec. exposures and combined them in Photoshop, enhancing natural colors of the stars using the Vibrance and Saturation sliders.*

STAR TRAILS

Star trails are a classic night photography subject and can make for compelling images, with individual stars appearing to streak across the night sky as Earth rotates. Alternatively, if you point your camera toward the North or South Pole and shoot a long exposure, the stars will appear to circle around a fixed point—this is the north celestial pole (NCP) in the Northern Hemisphere and the south celestial pole (SCP) in the Southern Hemisphere.

Your assignment is to capture a rotation of the stars around the NCP or SCP over a period of at least one hour, shooting multiple long exposures—6 images per minute, each with a 10 sec. exposure—and "stacking" them at the editing stage to capture the full drama of the trails. The NCP is very close to Polaris (also known as the North Star or Pole Star), which is on the tail of Ursa Minor (the Little Bear). The SCP is located within the boundaries of the Octans constellation, which is near the Crux constellation, and can be found by drawing an imaginary line along the longest arm of the Southern Cross (Crux's four main stars).

This assignment is best attempted on a clear night. Select your lens's widest aperture, keep ISO as low as possible, and program your remote shutter release to shoot at appropriate intervals. The longer the overall exposure, the more pronounced the star trails.

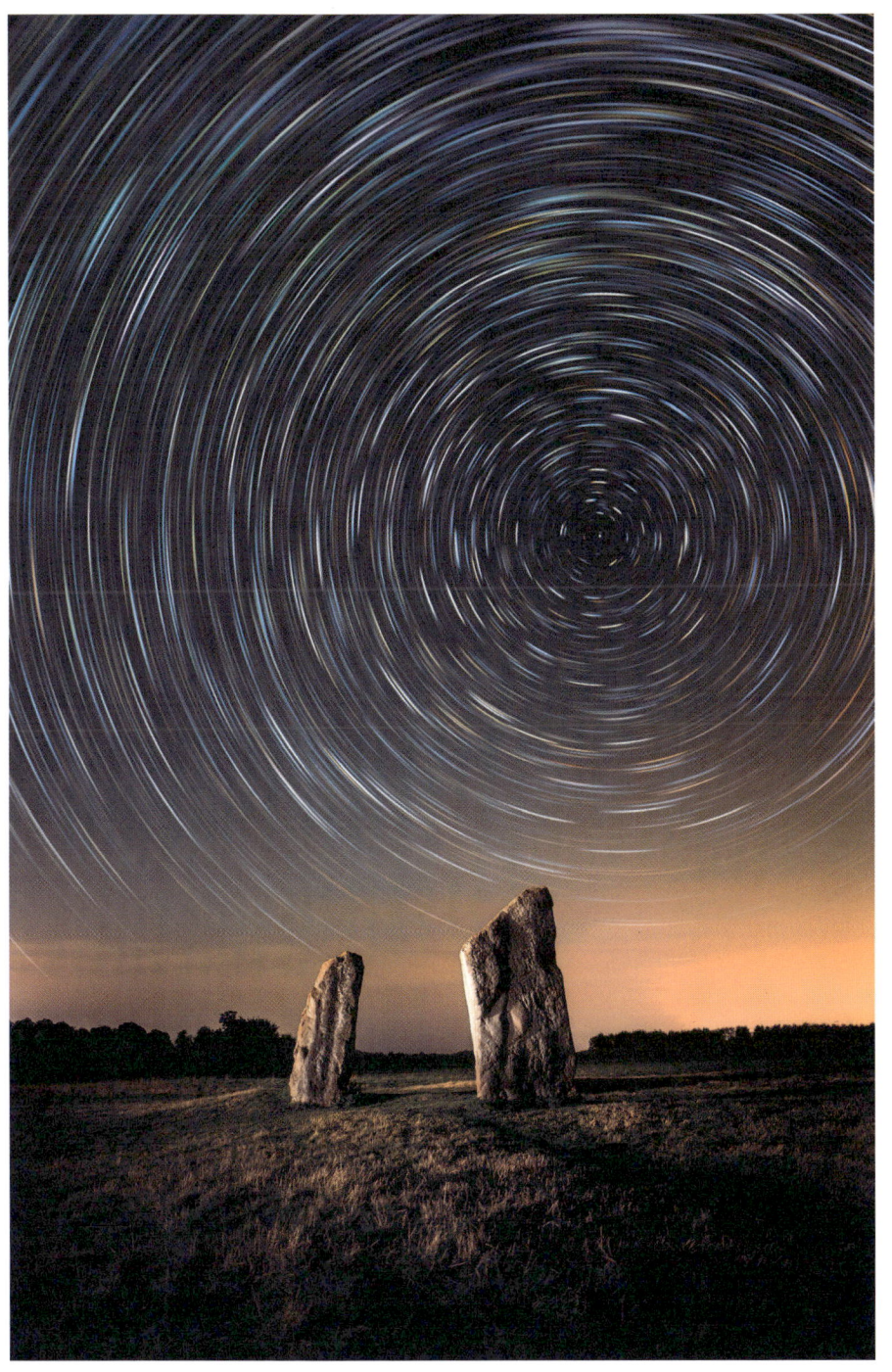

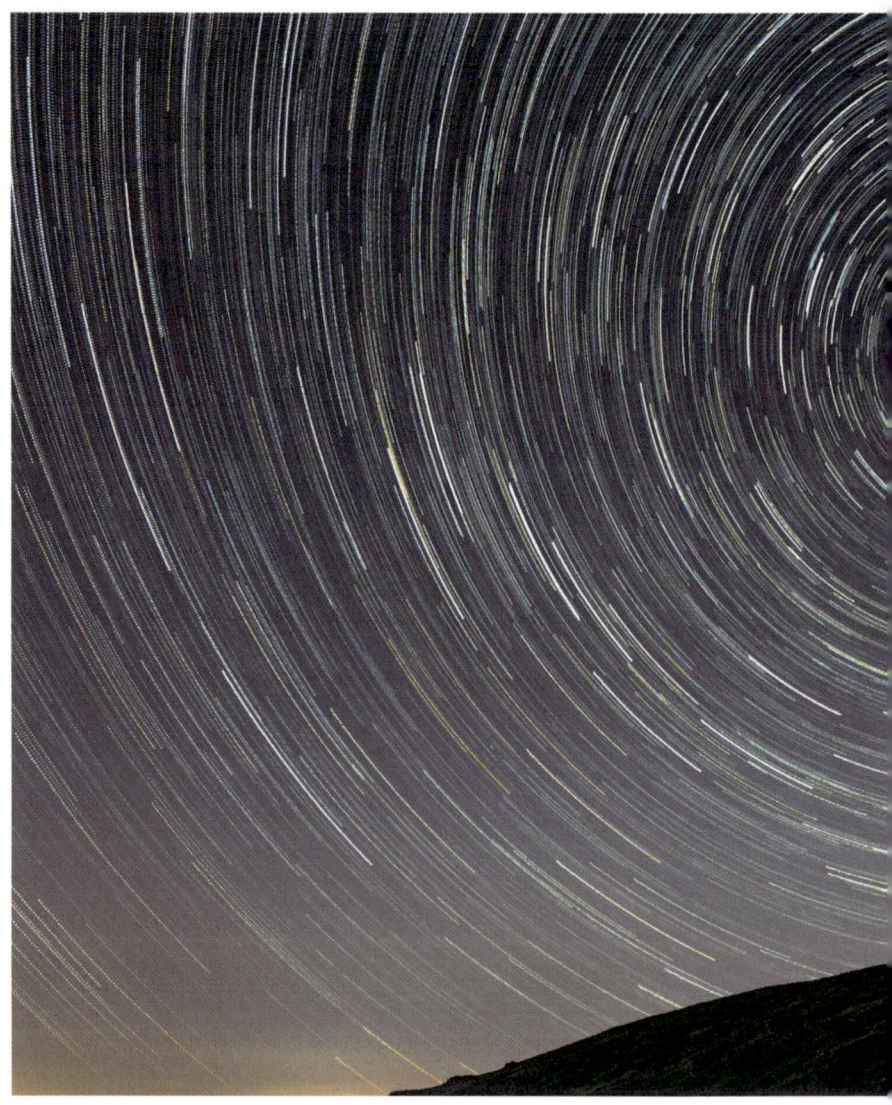

FIELD NOTES

Since star-trail images are created by stacking multiple long exposures rather than being a single shot, they could be considered to be synthetic. However, considering star-trail images can only be created from photographs you have composed and taken yourself, I feel they are valid artistically and they offer another perspective of the universe.

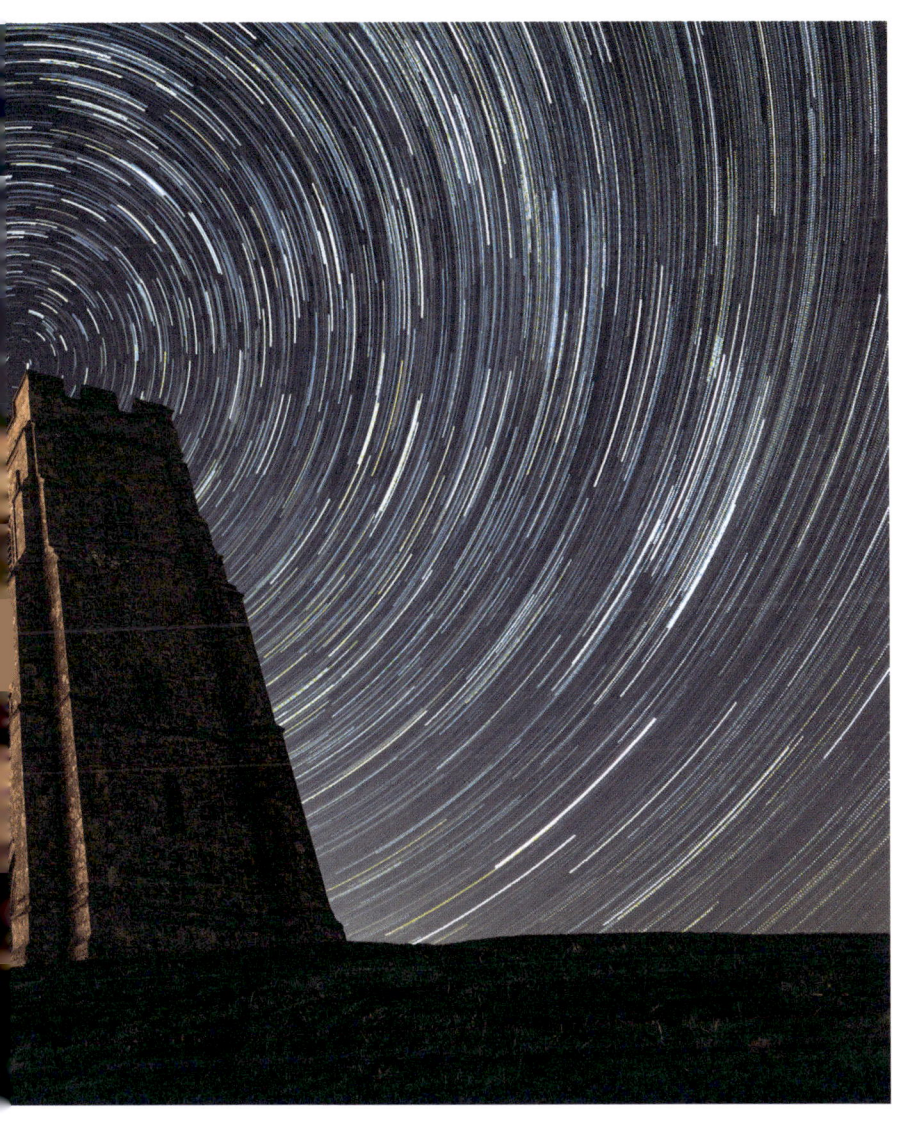

▲ The "sub" images used to create these dramatic star trails
were captured over a one-hour period.

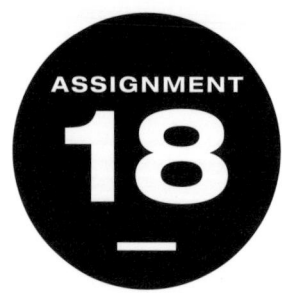

ASSIGNMENT

18

METEOR SHOWERS

Meteor showers occur when Earth passes through the trail of debris left by comets. This debris, often no larger than a grain of sand, burns up as it speeds through Earth's atmosphere at up to 30,000mph (48,280km/h), creating bright streaks of light in the night sky. Comets are some of the oldest objects in our solar system, so meteor showers are essentially spectacular ancient firework displays!

Your assignment is to capture a dramatic image of this cosmic light show. First, use your resources to find out when a meteor shower is likely to be visible. Meteor showers are annual events—for instance, the Perseid meteor shower occurs every August.

Once you've identified a suitable meteor shower, consider its intensity. Meteor showers comprise hundreds of objects, making for a stunning display. Typically, the Perseids in August and the Geminids in December are the most active. However, the weather and moon phase will determine how many meteors will be visible on a given night around the "peak" of the meteor shower.

Position your tripod low to the ground, select your lens's widest aperture, and aim for a shutter speed between 6 and 10 sec. To balance the exposure, set ISO to between 400 and 800. Attach your remote shutter release and set it to take continuous images. Aim your camera toward the "radiant" (the part of the sky where the shower appears to emanate from). Alternatively, point your camera away from the radiant and capture the shower as it "rains" down to Earth. Long-exposure photography increases your chances of capturing meteors.

TIPS

• Find a dark-sky location (see Assignment 37), as light pollution decreases the contrast of the night sky, reducing the number of meteors you see.

• If possible, time your shoot to coincide with a new moon, as this is when light pollution is at its least obstructive, allowing us to see more meteors.

• A prime lens of 20mm or wider will give you the greatest chance of capturing meteors, although any wideangle focal length will produce stunning results.

▶ *This composite image of the Perseid meteors was taken with a fisheye lens over a period of 3.5 hours.*

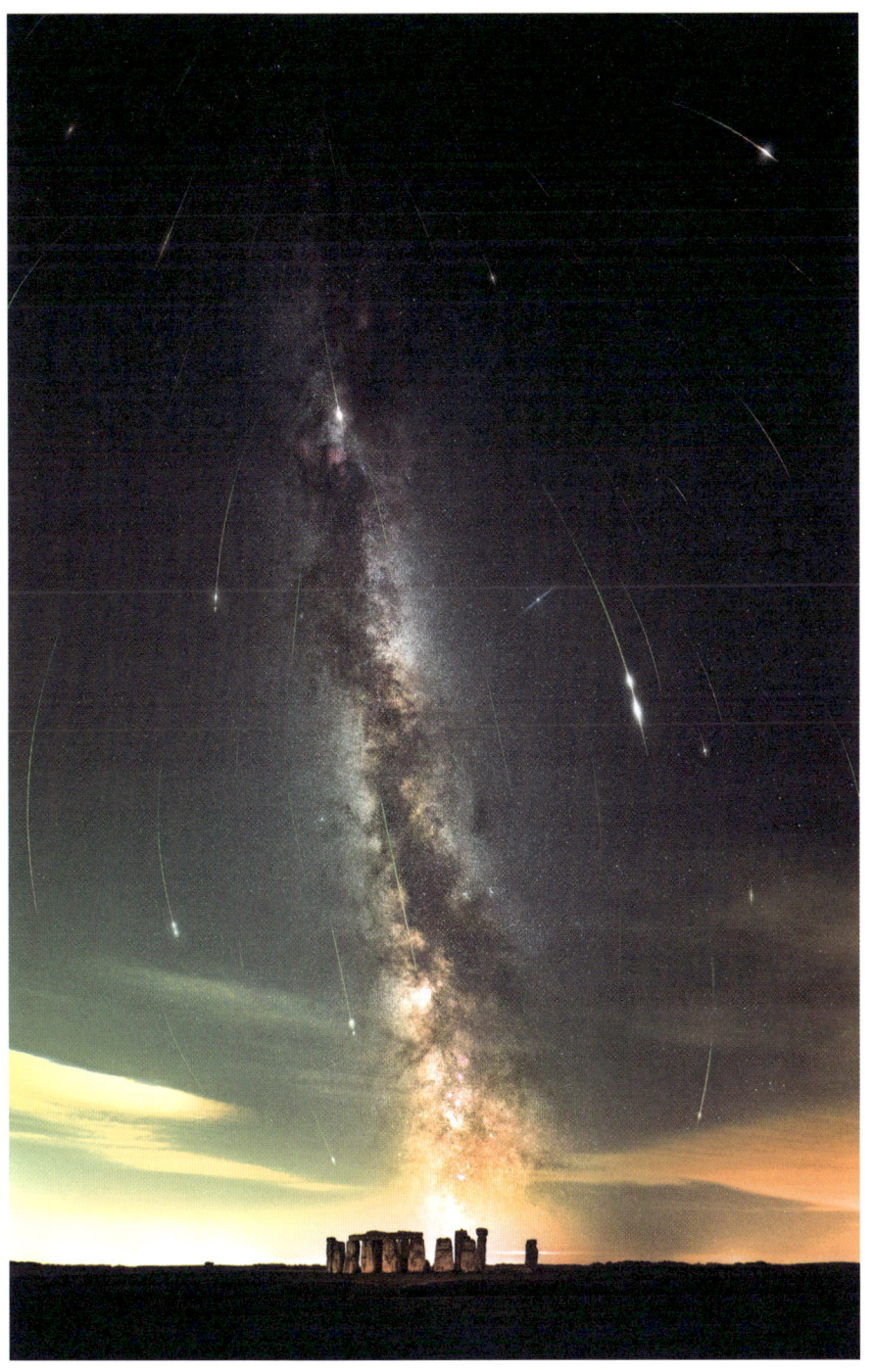

ASSIGNMENT

19

TIPS

- Most comets are faint and may only be visible through a camera. Scan the night sky with a wideangle lens and take a series of test shots to confirm the comet's location.

- Longer exposures may be needed for fainter comets, while shorter exposures may be needed for brighter comets.

COMETS

Comets are balls of ice and dust that orbit the sun and hold material from the early formation of our solar system 4.6 billion years ago. These frozen time capsules take hundreds to thousands of years to complete their orbits and, although unpredictable, roughly one per year is visible to the naked eye. Your assignment is to photograph one of these celestial visitors in a single frame.

Stellarium is an invaluable resource for locating comets, as you can use your GPS location to plot where a comet will be visible at a certain time. Depending on their closest approach to the sun, they can either appear just before dawn or after sunset. If possible, time your shoot to coincide with a new moon, as darker skies result in greater contrast, increasing your chances of seeing the comet. Could you add to the story by including subjects in your foreground that reflect the comet's age?

Keep your exposures below 8 sec. to avoid the effects of Earth's rotation and select a relatively high ISO. Use a wideangle lens if you want to include more of the landscape, or a telephoto lens if you want the comet to dominate the frame.

FIELD NOTES

Comets are composed of different materials, which react when they are heated by the sun. Some release gases that produce classic "tails," while others develop a bright "nucleus" (the solid center). Comets are notoriously unpredictable, so keep a close eye on them and see how they appear in the night sky.

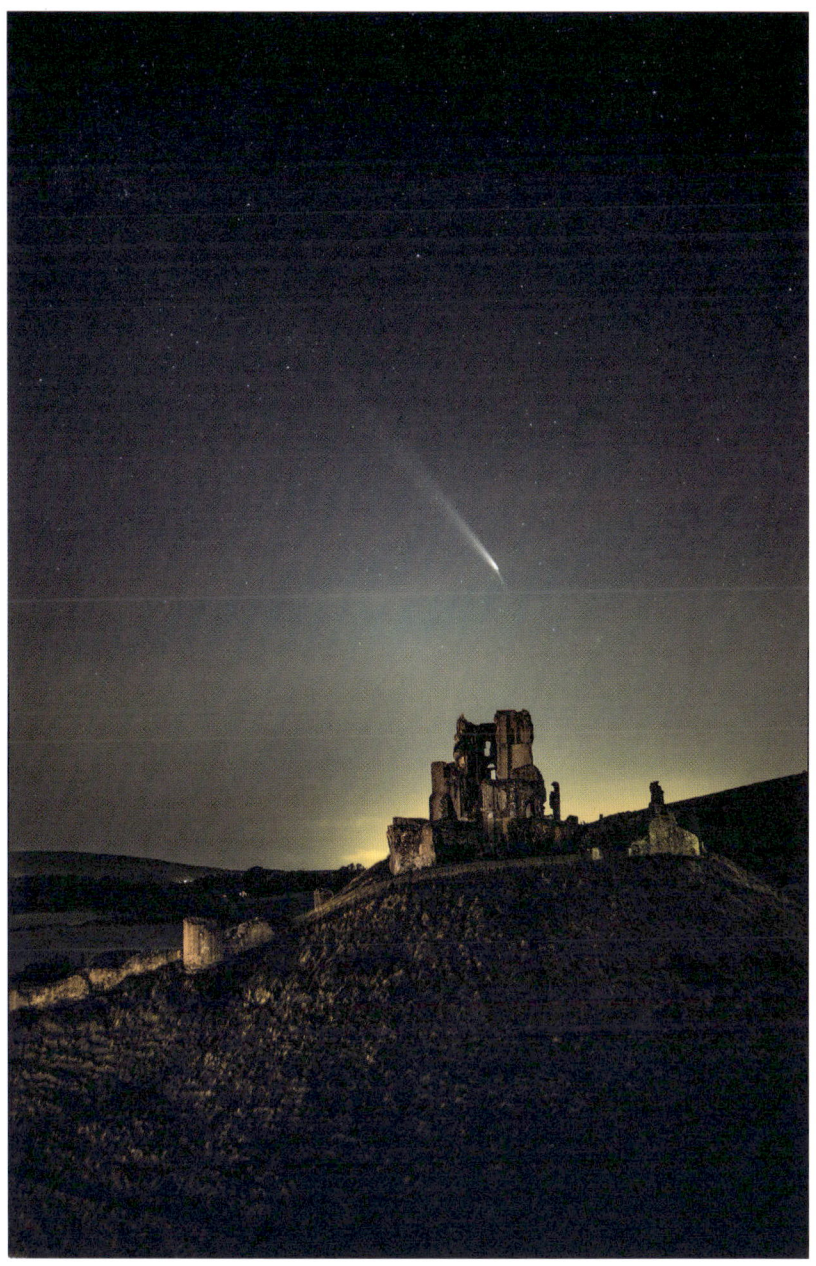

▲ *The ruins of Corfe Castle provide the perfect foreground for this image of the C/2023 A3 (Tsuchinshan–ATLAS) comet. While the castle is almost 1,000 years old, the comet is one of the oldest objects in the entire solar system.*

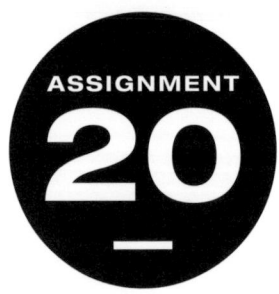

ASSIGNMENT
20

TIPS

- Take warm clothing and provisions with you. This may be a long shoot, so be prepared.

- The color of a totally eclipsed moon can change from one event to the next depending on what is happening in Earth's atmosphere at the time. Not only is this a creative image, it's a scientific one too.

▶ *This image captures a partial lunar eclipse over a four-hour period, illustrating the interaction of Earth's shadow with the surface of the moon.*

LUNAR ECLIPSE

A lunar eclipse occurs when Earth perfectly aligns itself between the sun and moon, blocking light from the sun and casting its shadow onto the moon. Depending on how much of the moon is in shadow, it may look as though a bite has been taken out of its surface. When the moon is totally eclipsed, light is scattered through Earth's atmosphere, with beautiful red, orange, and sometimes blue hues appearing. These spectacular events only happen during a full moon and, unlike a solar eclipse, are safe to view with the naked eye. Your assignment is to photograph a lunar eclipse from beginning to end, blending multiple frames into a single image.

Photographing a lunar eclipse is much the same as photographing the moon (see Assignment 4), with just a few technical tweaks. You will need a lens with a focal length of 400mm or greater. To capture the "umbral" shadow in greater clarity, exposures times will need to be between 1/400 sec. and 2 sec. Lunar eclipses can last for several hours, so if possible, use a star tracker and keep your camera tracking the moon for the duration of the event.

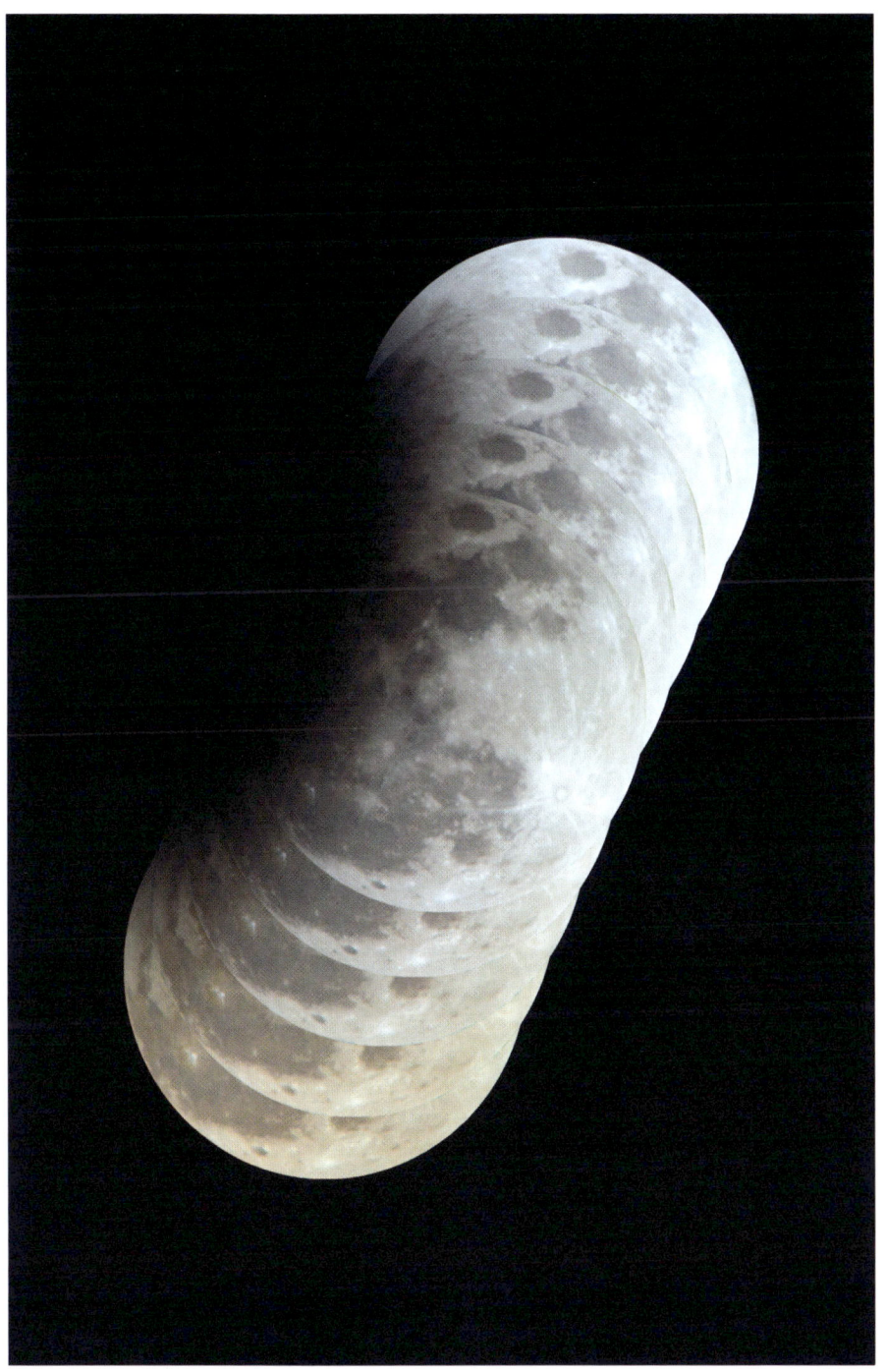

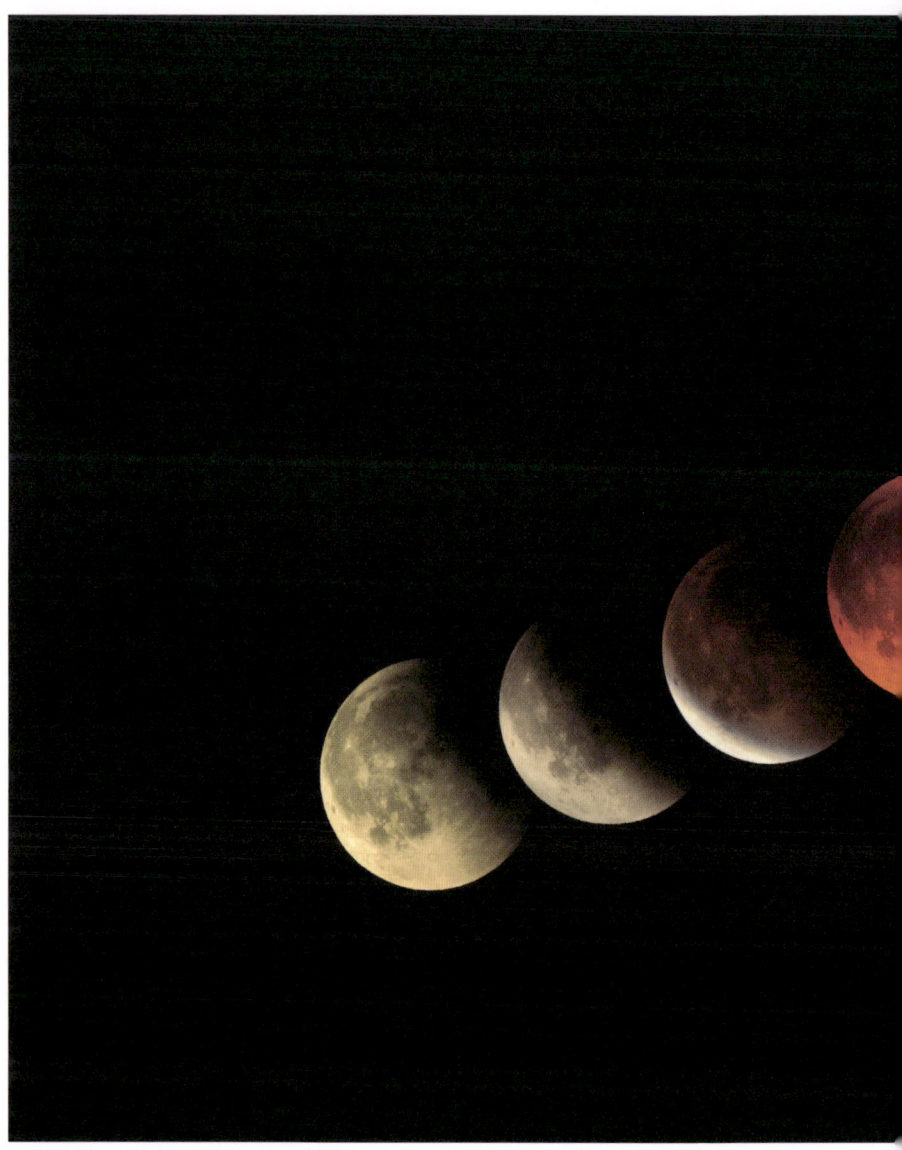

FIELD NOTES

A great online resource for predicting lunar eclipses is www.timeanddate.com. Click on the Sun, Moon & Space tab, then select Eclipses from the drop-down menu and search by city, country, or year. The website lists forthcoming eclipses alongside path maps and 3D path globes. All you need now is a clear sky.

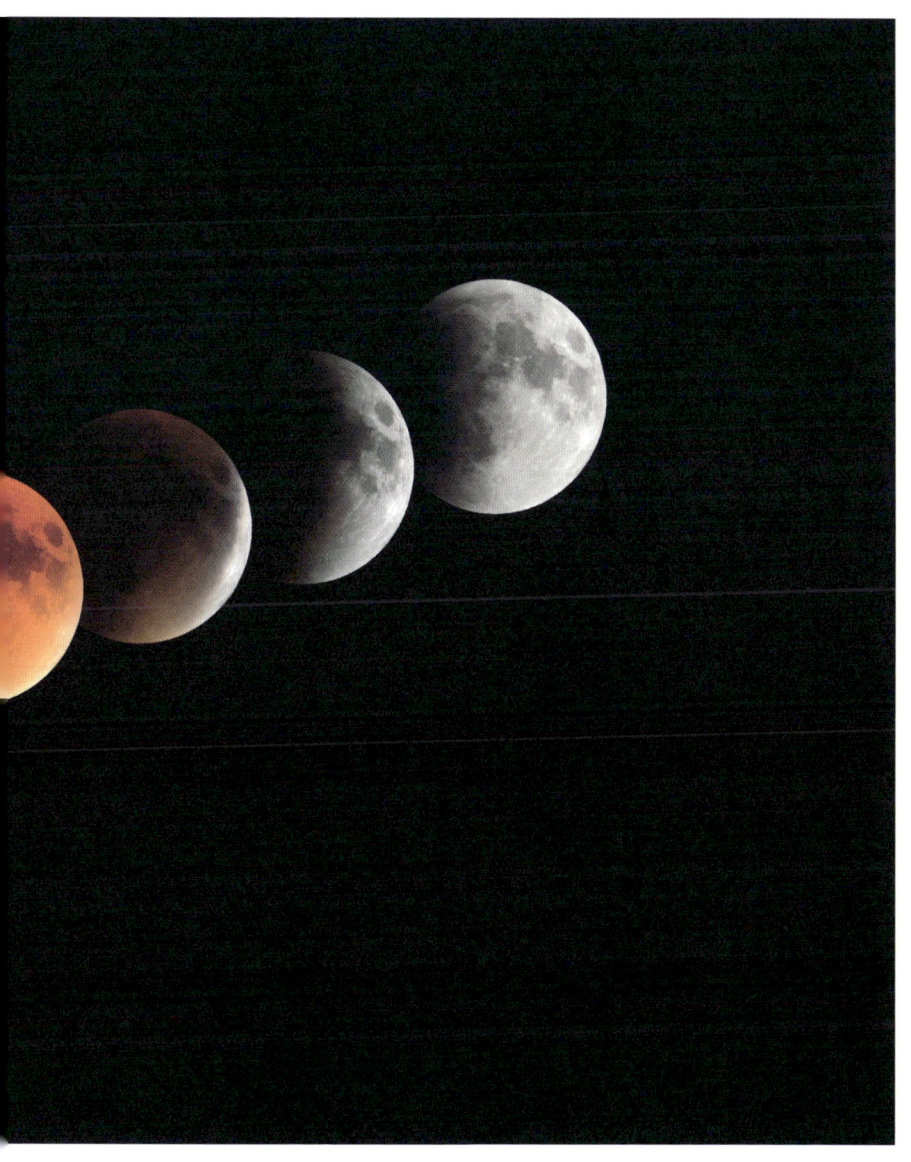

▲ *This composite image of a total lunar eclipse uses long exposures to capture the refracted moonlight.*

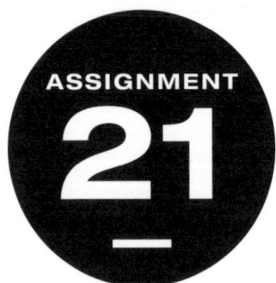

ASSIGNMENT
21

TIPS

- Set a series of alarms at key times during the eclipse to remind you how much time you have left to acquire your photos.

- Use a star tracker for exposures of up to 10 sec.—you don't want blurry images of an eclipse!

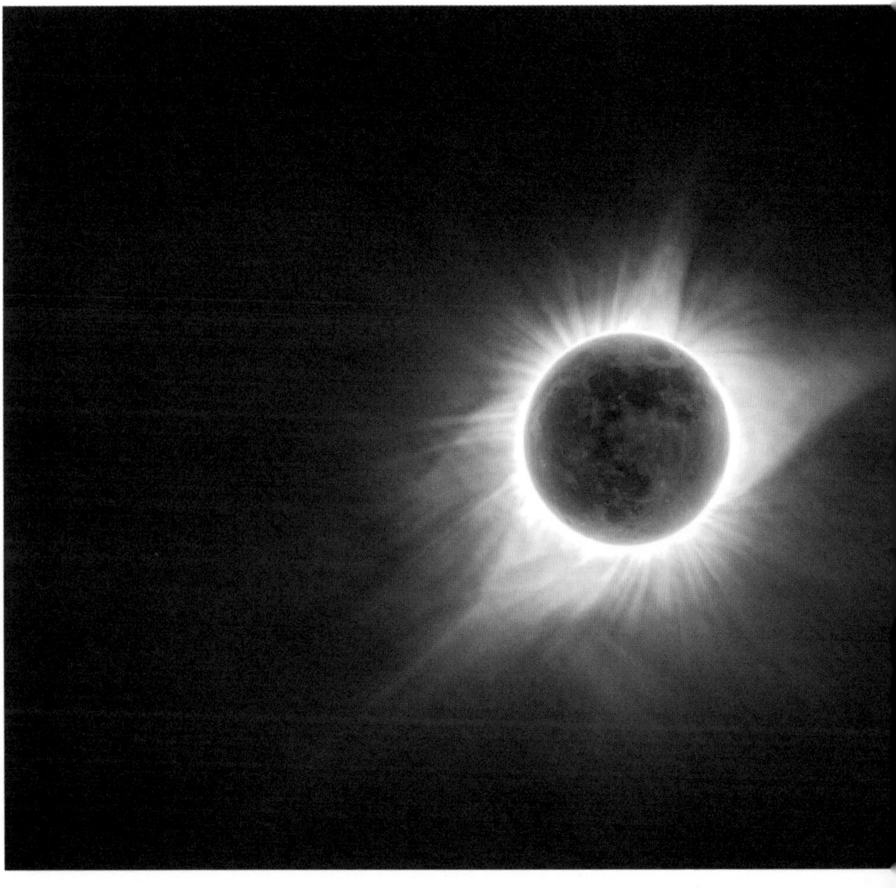

TOTAL SOLAR ECLIPSE

When the moon passes between Earth and the sun, it blocks the light of the sun from reaching Earth, causing a total solar eclipse (when the sun, moon, and Earth are perfectly aligned) or partial solar eclipse (when they are not perfectly aligned). These magical events happen every 18 months across Earth and, unlike lunar eclipses, only last for a few minutes, which means that photographing one requires planning and preparation.

Your mission is to find the next "path of totality" (the area where a total eclipse can be viewed) near you, mark the date in your diary, and capture this once-in-a-lifetime event. Only a partial solar eclipse will be visible outside this zone. A great resource for finding future eclipses is www.timeanddate.com, which uses your location to give precise dates and details. Click on the Sun, Moon & Space dropdown menu, select the Eclipses option and enter a location or year to get started.

A total solar eclipse is the only time it is safe to point your lens at the sun, and I would recommend a telephoto of 200mm or more to reveal the sun's outer atmosphere, known as the corona. Trial a series of exposures from 1-10 sec. to capture the varying surface brightness of the outer corona. Be aware that the temperature will drop suddenly during a total solar eclipse, and you will be temporarily plunged into darkness.

◀ A high dynamic range (HDR) image of a total solar eclipse photographed in Nashville, Tennessee.

FIELD NOTES

It is *never* safe to look directly at the sun with the naked eye or through a camera without proper eye protection because its light can permanently damage the retina. Instead, invest in a solar filter, which blocks out 99.999 percent of light for safe solar observation. Once the "diamond ring" effect becomes visible at the end of a totality, attach your solar filter immediately.

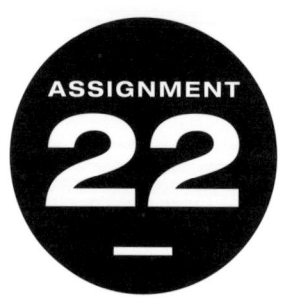

ASSIGNMENT

22

TIPS

- Aurora apps are not 100-percent accurate and only provide a prediction. Patience is key to aurora success.

- Geomagnetic storms can hit at any time after dark, so be prepared to travel at any time of the night.

- Auroras can understandably be popular events. Refer to Assignment 50 if you intend to photograph a well-known location.

▶ *Depending on where you are in the world, auroras can be rare occurrences, so don't miss out on the chance to document these mesmerizing events with your camera.*

AURORAS

Auroras are one of Earth's most beautiful atmospheric phenomena. These dancing ribbons of light occur when energized particles from the sun slam into Earth's upper atmosphere at up to 45 million mph (72 million km/h) and are redirected toward the poles by Earth's magnetic field. Aurora hotspots include Iceland, Norway, Canada, and New Zealand. However, increased activity around the solar maximum often means they can be seen at much lower latitudes. For this assignment, you're going to be capturing your own aurora images.

It is crucial to know when and where auroras are likely to appear. Satellites monitor solar wind signals and there are several apps that predict such events. My favorite app is Aurora, as not only does it feature an aurora map, but it also provides a long-term forecast. You also need clear skies, so use your weather apps to plan accordingly.

Arrive at your location in plenty of time and keep your eyes peeled for faint pillars of reds and greens, as these are often the first tell-tale signs of an aurora. Be flexible when it comes to composition and be prepared to move your setup at a moment's notice—aurora can appear just above the horizon or directly overhead, depending on where you are in the world. Auroras can also be intense, but how brightly they appear in a photograph depends on how much light you let into your camera. Start with a shutter speed of 5 sec. and set ISO to its lowest value to preserve detail.

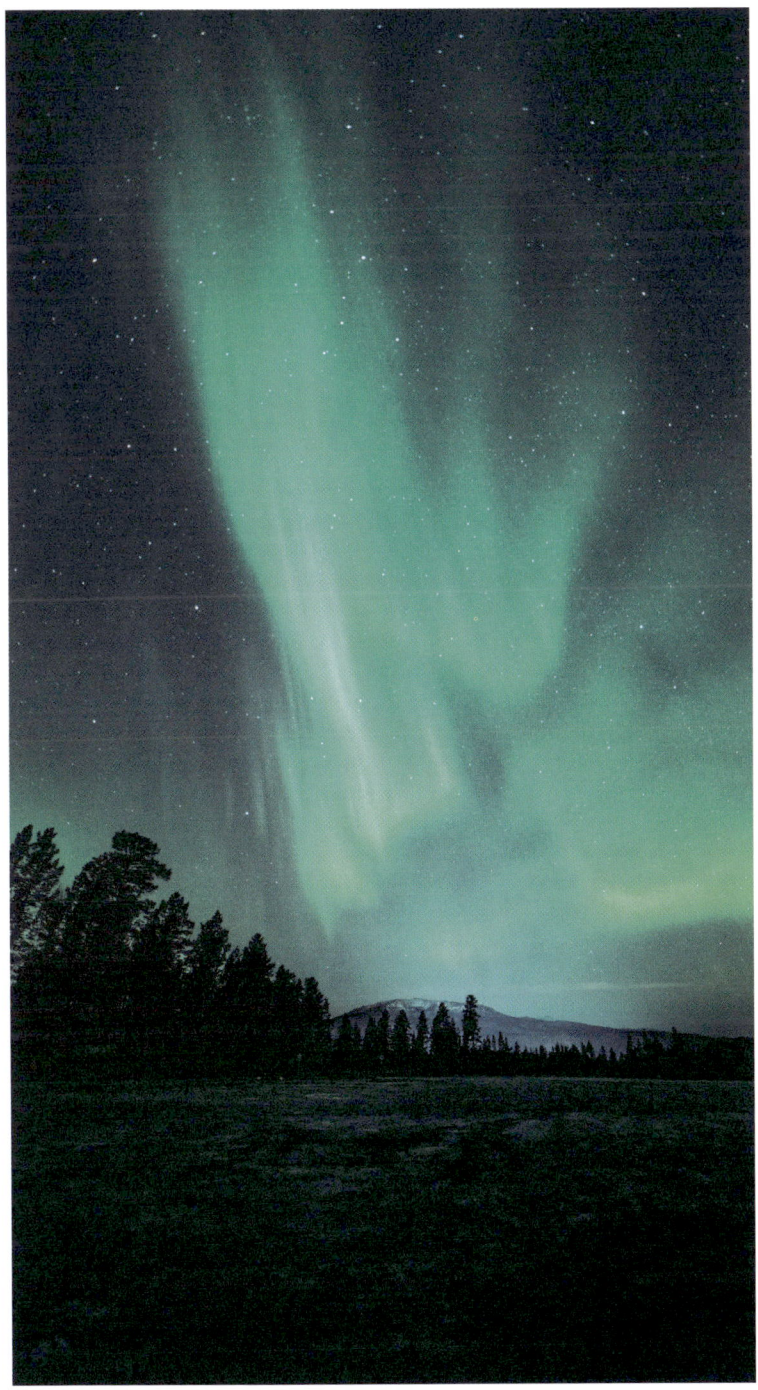

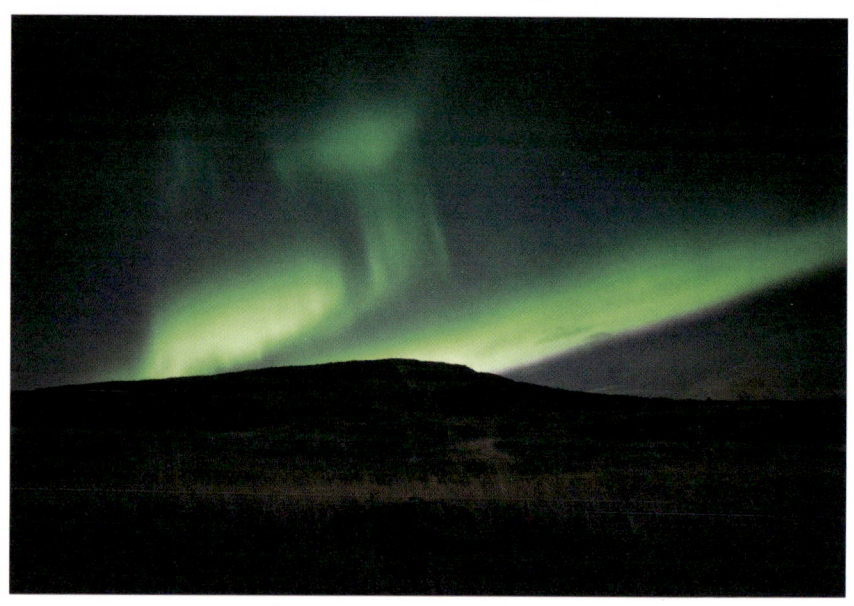

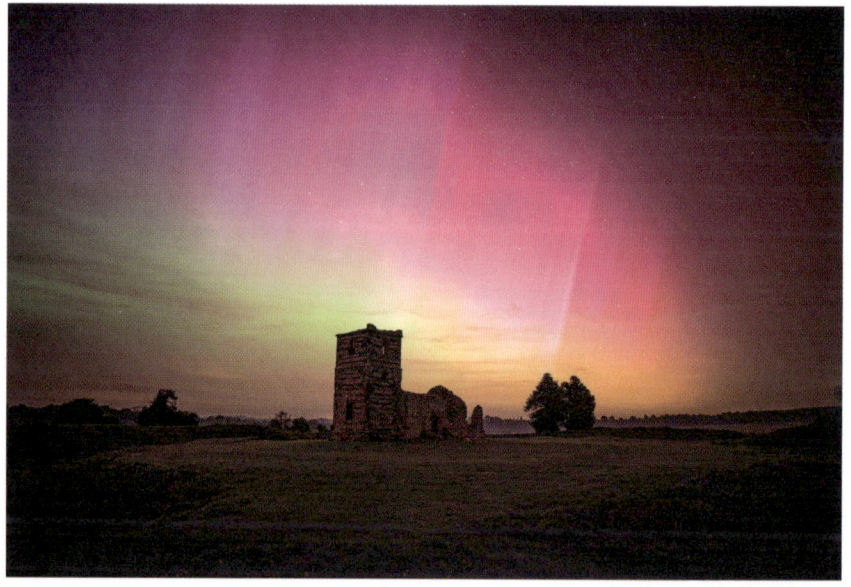

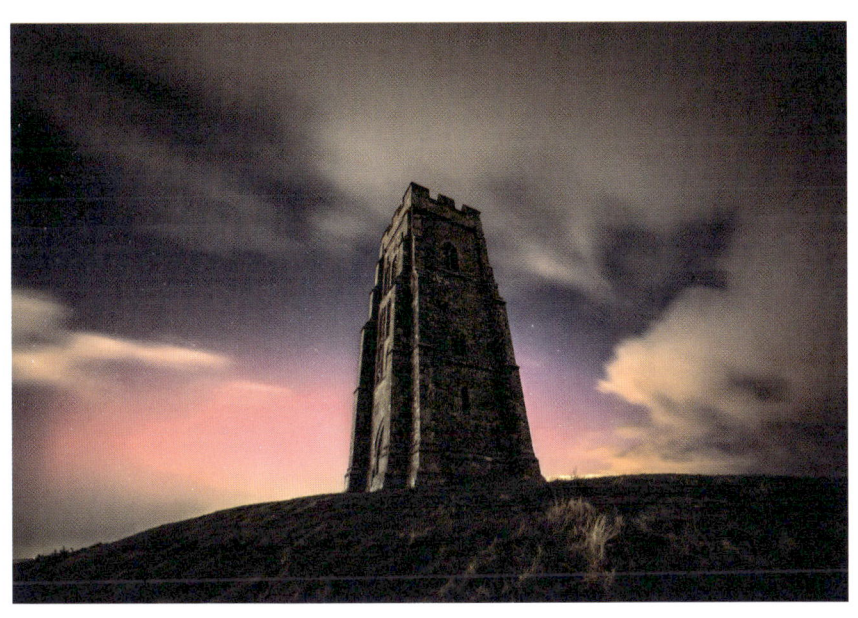

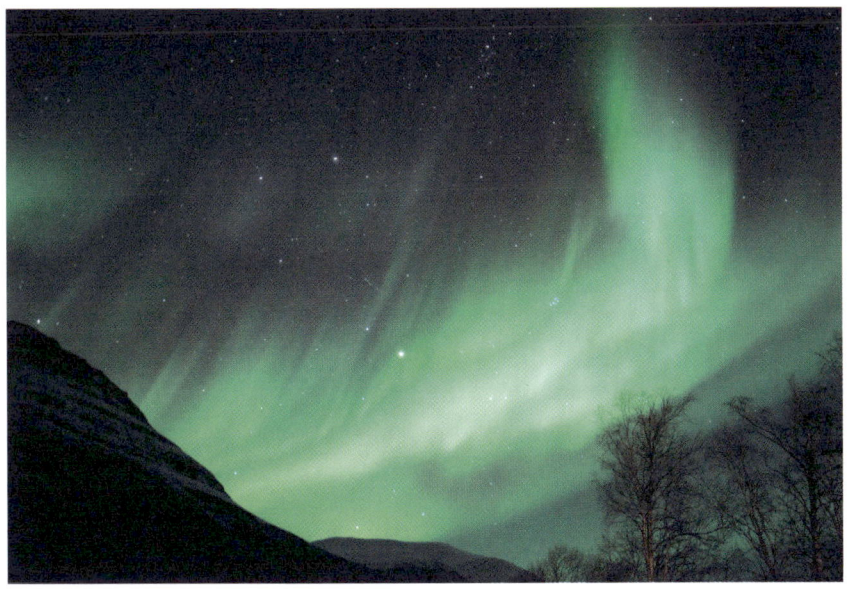

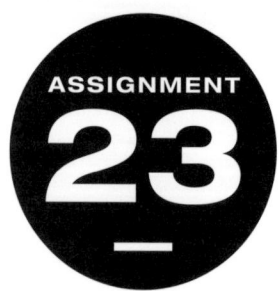

ASSIGNMENT
23

TIPS

- Check a light-pollution map such as www.lightpollutionmap.info and select areas with a low Bortle number.

- Some coastal areas offer designated paths and parking areas. Do your research before venturing out.

▶ *I captured this dramatic image of the Milky Way low on the local horizon from Portland Bill.*

OUT TO SEA

Light pollution is as much of a problem in coastal areas as it is in inland towns and cities, with artificial light disrupting the ocean's natural rhythms and threatening marine habitats. But if you can find a dark-sky site at the coast, ideally lower than Bortle 3–4 and overlooking the ocean, you can use the sea to add an extra layer of interest to your night-sky images.

For this assignment, head to the coast and shoot a seascape at night using the ebb and flow of an incoming tide, rock formations, or a lighthouse to anchor your shot and provide foreground interest. Fill the sky with a suitably vast subject such as the Milky Way, constellations, comets, meteor showers, or even the Rho Ophiuchi cloud complex (only visible to the naked eye from dark-sky locations).

Health and safety should always be your first priority when shooting in any coastal location. Check the tide times and your location's accessibility in advance and pay attention to any warning signs for rip tides and quicksand. It's also a good idea to Geotag your location and let someone know where you are in case of an emergency.

To capture the motion of waves washing over rocks, start with a shutter speed of 8 sec. and select an ISO of around 640. If there are any boats or other sources of light out to sea, you may have to reduce your exposure times to avoid overexposure.

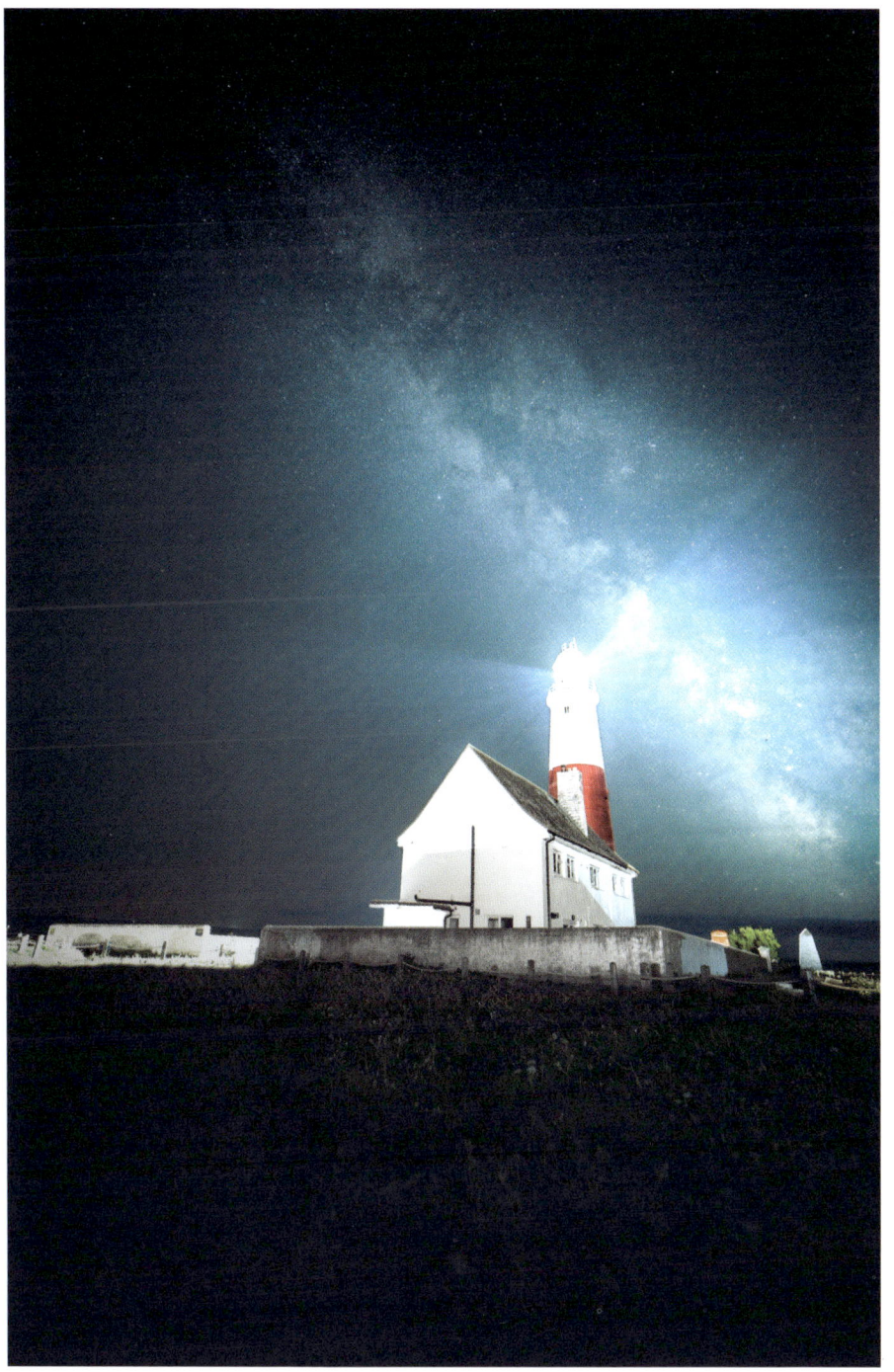

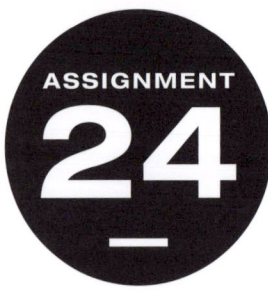

ASSIGNMENT
24
—

TIPS

• Travel light—you only need a camera, lens, and tripod. There's nothing worse than taking a full kit bag to the beach only to risk it being soaked by the incoming tide.

• Always be aware of tide times and ensure you have a safe escape route so you are not cut off by the incoming tide.

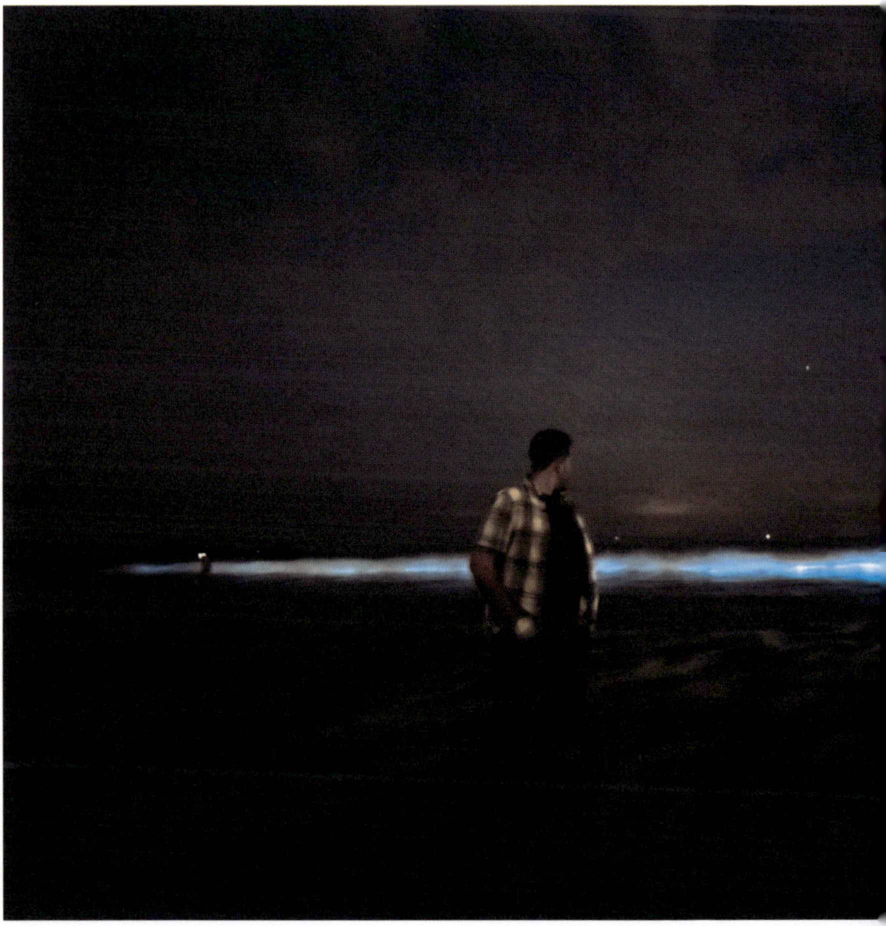

BIOLUMINESCENT PLANKTON

During the summer months, something utterly magical happens in the lapsing waves along certain stretches of coastline at night: waves start to glow with a neon-blue intensity, announcing the presence of bioluminescent plankton—small marine organisms that produce light through chemical reactions, causing the surface of the ocean to sparkle.

For this assignment, try capturing your own bioluminescent seascapes. You don't need to travel far to see this wonder of the natural world—sightings have been reported along the south coast of the UK, the Maldives, stretches of the west coast of the USA, and Australia—and there are numerous social media groups that report sightings and recommend locations. Search "bioluminescence plankton watch."

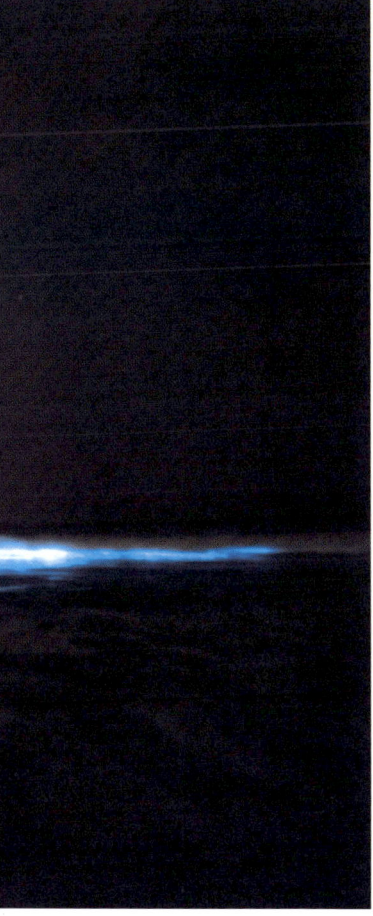

Photographing bioluminescent plankton is easier than you might imagine. Look for a clear sky, a new moon (light from the moon will reduce contrast), and a high tide. Use a wideangle lens for a contextualized shot and an ISO of 800, and keep exposure times to 6–8 sec. to avoid overexposing the bioluminescence. You could even include the Milky Way.

◄ *This very strong plumage of bioluminescent plankton was captured off the coast of South Wales. Not only did it show up vibrantly on camera, it was easily discernible to the naked eye.*

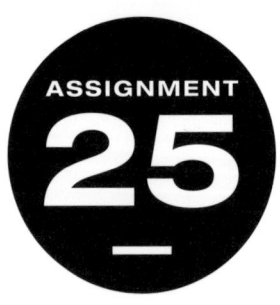

ASSIGNMENT
25

TIPS

- As the subject here is the lunar halo, the moon itself will be overexposed, so choose an exposure that distinguishes the halo from the background sky.

- Shoot in portrait orientation to capture a more compelling scene with greater emphasis on the sky and moon halo.

▶ *The light from the moon scattered through Earth's atmosphere makes for dreamlike nightscape images.*

MOON HALO

Have you ever seen a glowing ring around the moon? This optical illusion is known as a moon halo, or lunar halo, and is caused by the refraction of moonlight from hexagonal ice crystals in the upper atmosphere. On rare occasions, you may even be lucky enough to see a double halo around the moon.

Halos are more common during the fall and winter months when there is a greater moisture content in Earth's atmosphere. Unlike most other astronomical events and objects, this is one effect best viewed when a full (or nearly full) moon is veiled by thin cirrus clouds. These clouds are transparent and cover huge areas of the sky and produce a variety of halo-like effects.

Your assignment is to capture a lunar halo around the time of a full moon. Select a wideangle lens, keep your aperture wide and your ISO low, and set a shutter speed of 5–10 sec. Alternatively, create a dramatic "starburst" effect by using a narrow aperture and a longer shutter speed.

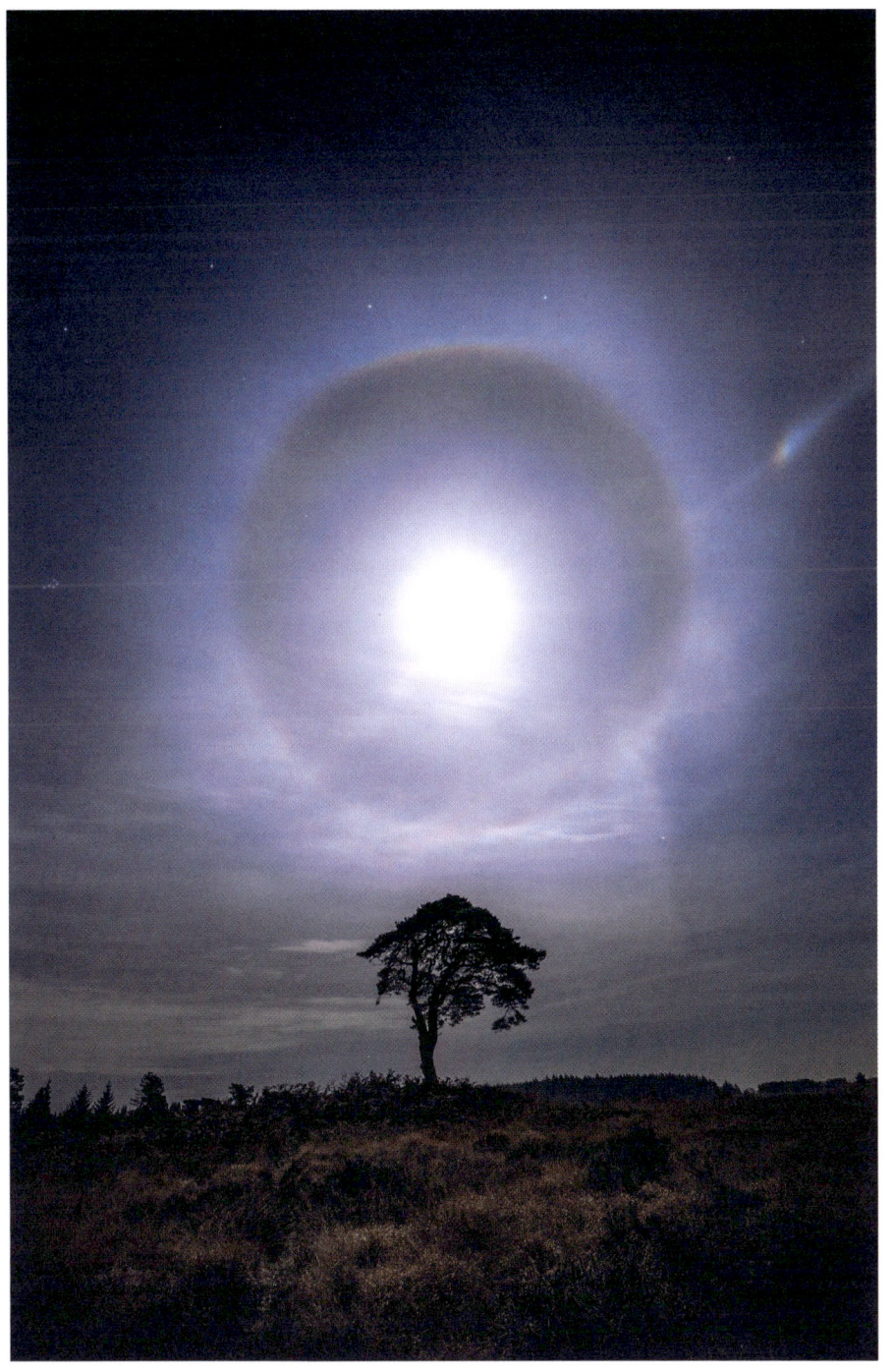

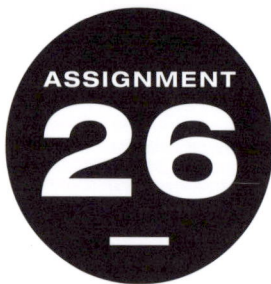

ASSIGNMENT
26

TIPS

- Scattered light is very faint, although the signal can be enhanced by applying a subtle Curves or Contrast adjustment to your images in post-production.

- Increase the Clarity slider to enhance the contrast between the stars and the airglow.

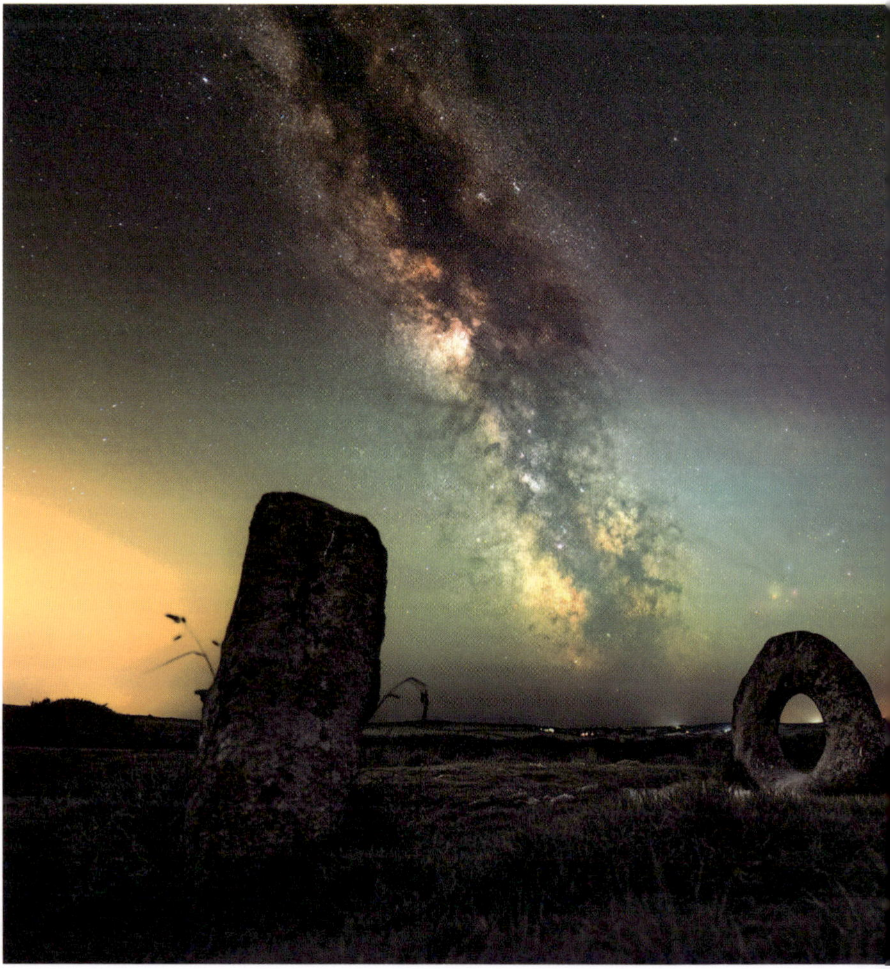

AIRGLOW

Airglow occurs when atoms and molecules in the upper atmosphere emit light to shed excess energy, resulting in a diffuse glow, usually in green or red hues, and is visible on dark nights anywhere on Earth.

Airglow is typically detected at high ISOs, so for this assignment, start at ISO 1000 and aim to capture this phenomenon next time you are out shooting landscapes at night on or around a new moon. A shutter speed of 8 sec. should be enough to capture a faint structure—look for its colorful swathes of light among the stars.

◀ *Airglow turns the sky a beautiful turquoise-green at Mên-an-Tol in Cornwall.*

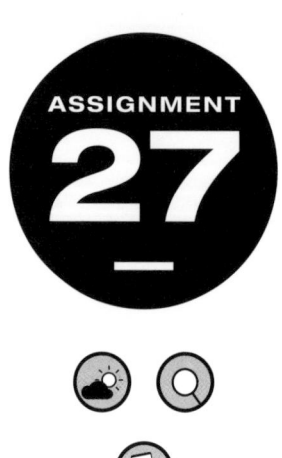

ASSIGNMENT
27

TIPS

- Noctilucent clouds can form and merge throughout the night. As a result, they can appear to the west after sunset and toward the east before sunrise.

- These cloud formations have a low surface brightness and are therefore difficult to focus on. Instead, focus on brighter stars or subjects on the local horizon.

▶ *A strong display of noctilucent clouds. I used a focal length of 85mm to capture the structure in the clouds, shown in close-up below.*

NOCTILUCENT CLOUDS

Noctilucent clouds are rare high-altitude clouds seen during clear summer nights at about the same time as the brightest stars become visible. Also known as "night-shining" clouds, they often appear as thin streaks, are reflective due to the angle of sunlight reaching them, and are usually blue or silver in color. Brighter displays are visible with the naked eye and appear like ghostly objects low to the horizon.

Although the appearance of noctilucent clouds is difficult to predict, finding a location with a flat horizon and a clear view of a large area of sky can increase your chances. Gaze up into the sky an hour or two after sunset or before sunrise. Cloud watchers will post about sightings on social media, so search for hashtags such as #noctilucentclouds to stay up to date.

To retain the maximum amount of detail, start with an ISO of 500 and a wide aperture and shoot a series of test exposures at 1 sec. and 2 sec. Push ISO further if you need to let more light in. Experiment with a range of lenses and focal lengths—noctilucent clouds vary in intensity and being able to work different compositions will increase your creative options.

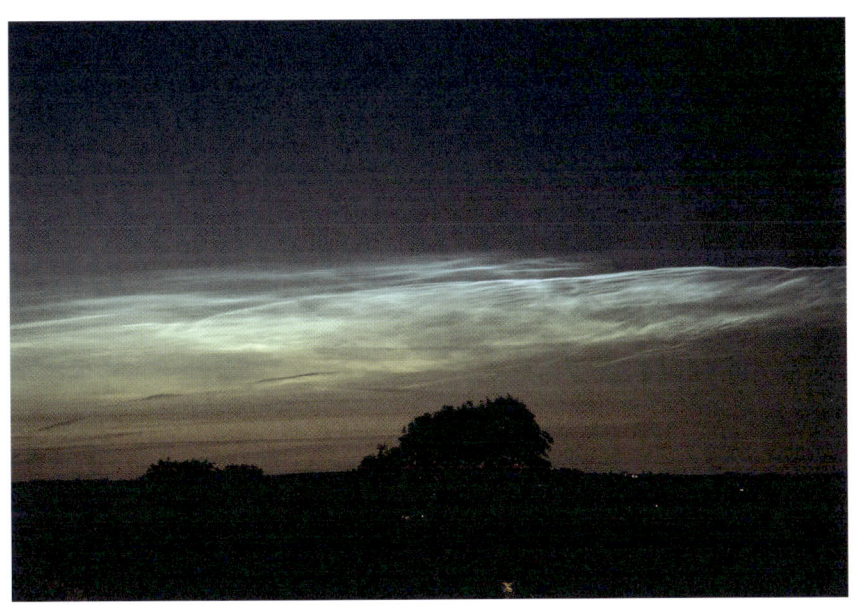

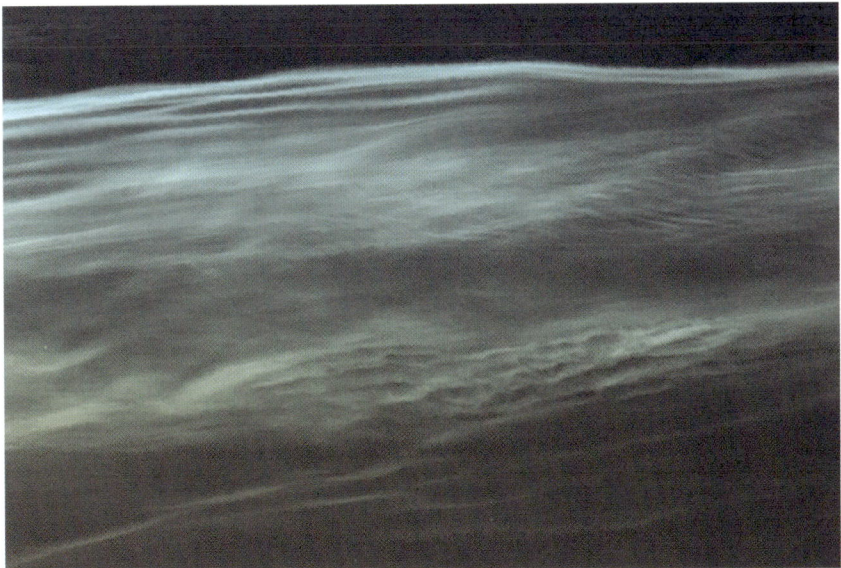

Noctilucent clouds close-up

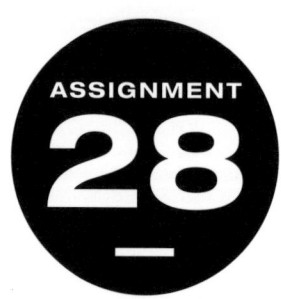

ASSIGNMENT
28
—

TIPS

- Aim to be in position at least one hour before sunrise to capture the start of the blue hour. Use your astronomy apps to work out precise timings.

- The more dramatic images tend to come as the dawn light emerges on the local horizon. For a moment, it is possible to capture the light of day and night in a single frame.

BEFORE THE DAWN

As dawn approaches, the rising sun scatters blue light across the sky creating a mood of mystery and serenity. Despite its name, the "blue hour" only lasts for 20–30 minutes, so to capture this softer, subtler light, you need to be in position at least an hour before sunrise. Your assignment is to capture a starry blue-hour nightscape that incorporates either the moon, a constellation, or the Milky Way.

As more light enters the frame, you will begin to lose detail in the sky, so start shooting the moment dawn breaks to reveal those bluish tones. Use the same exposure settings as you would for shooting the Milky Way (see Assignment 13) as dawn emerges and only start dialing back ISO as the light increases. As the stars fade, decrease your shutter speed.

▶ *As dawn approaches, a petroglyph looks up at the vanishing light of the Milky Way.*

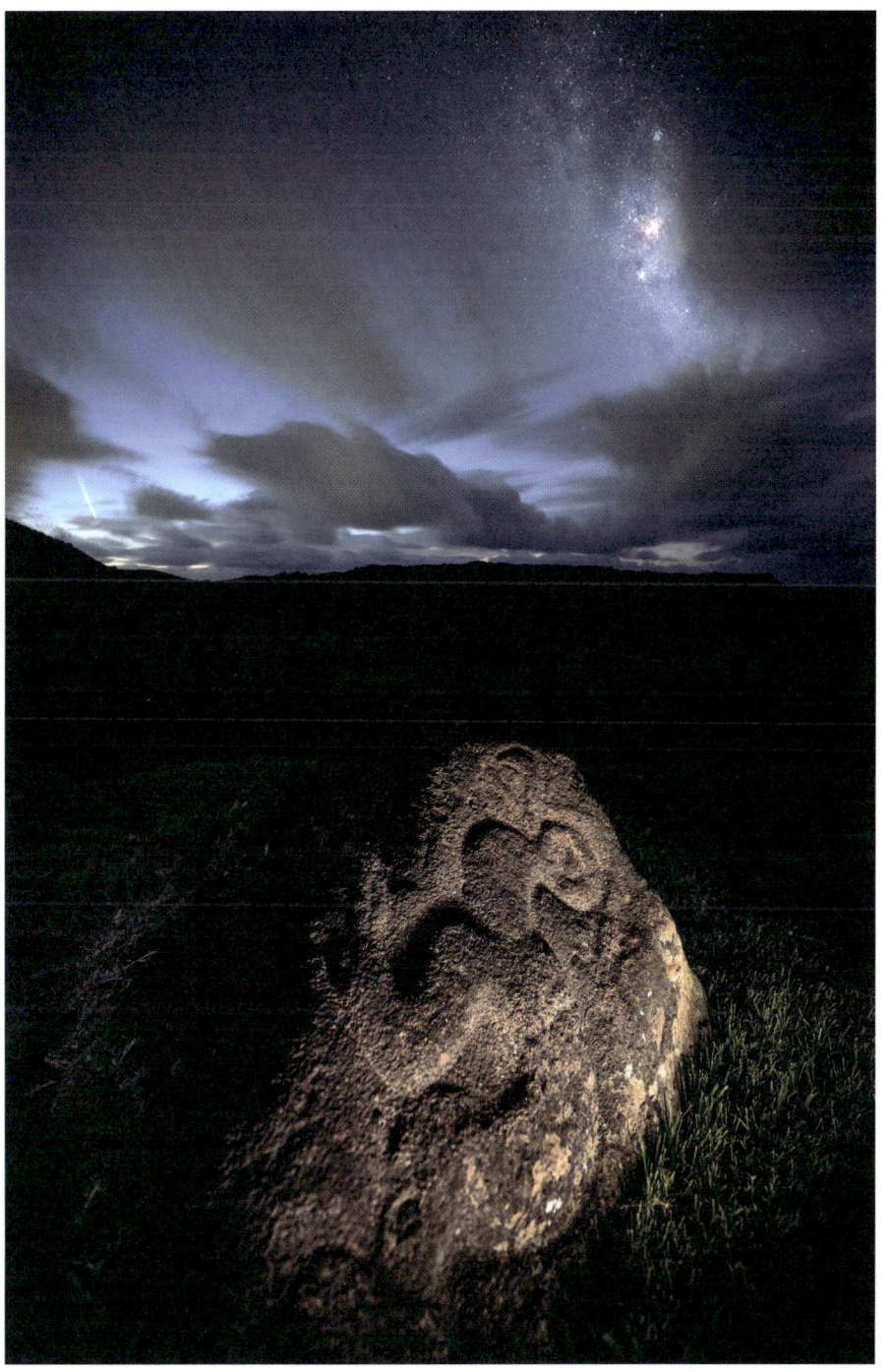

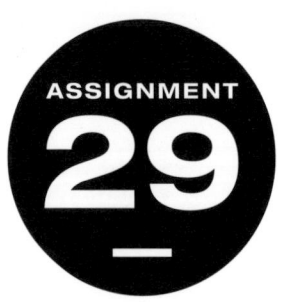

ASSIGNMENT
29

TIPS

- Use your tripod's built-in spirit level to make sure the tracker is level to either the northern/southern or celestial plane so it will track the correct celestial plane.

- It is useful to know your location's latitude when performing a polar alignment. In Google Maps, click on your location, round up the number, and adjust the latitude of your tracker accordingly.

- Fine-tune your alignment using the star tracker's Right Ascension (RA) and Declination (Dec.) movements.

▶ *Star trackers allow you to capture faint details over much longer periods of time than is possible without one, enabling you to use longer exposures and lower ISO values.*

STAR TRACKING

Star trackers need to be aligned to the north or south celestial pole through a process known as "polar alignment." In the Northern Hemisphere, this requires an alignment with the North Star, known as Polaris. In the Southern Hemisphere, the constellations Octans and Crux can be used.

There are several apps that simplify the polar-alignment process; one of the best is Star Adventurer Console, which uses a "polar clock" utility to find the exact location of the relevant celestial pole. Once centered, turn on your star tracker and select tracking for either the north or celestial pole. Polar alignment is now complete.

For this assignment, perform a polar alignment, mount your camera using a ball head adapter, and capture a single exposure of a bright star using a shutter speed of 10 sec. or more. This exercise will demonstrate the importance of using a star tracker when shooting long exposures of the night sky.

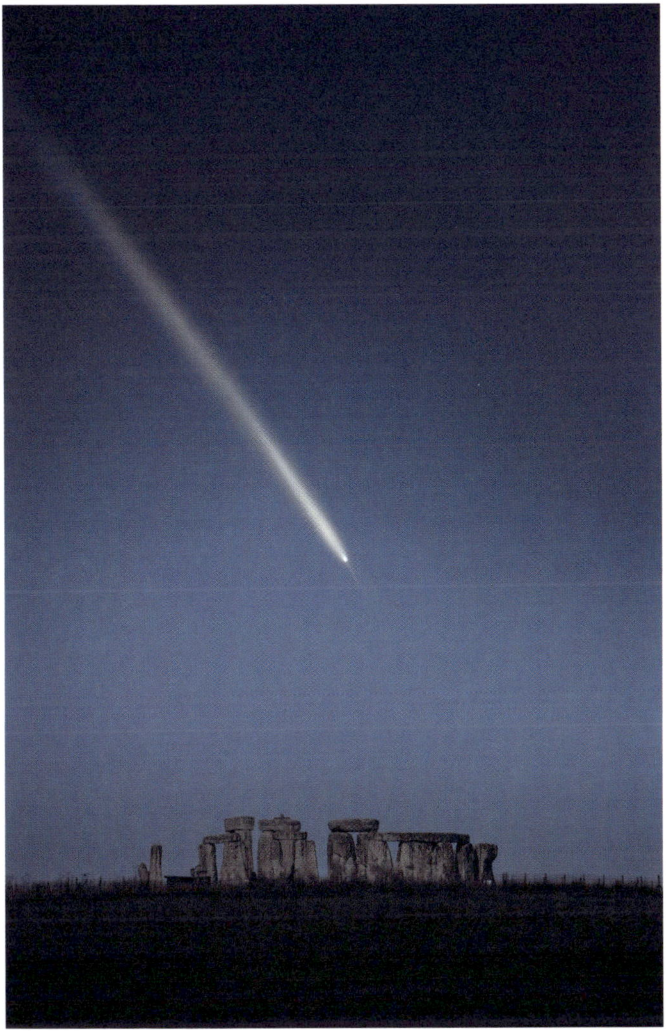

FIELD NOTES

The weight of your camera and lens can affect your alignment, so make sure your equipment falls within your tracker's payload limitations and check your alignment a few times before taking your images.

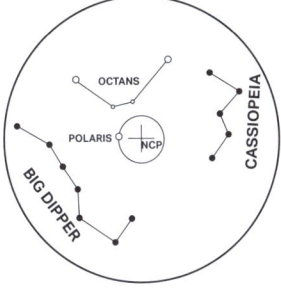

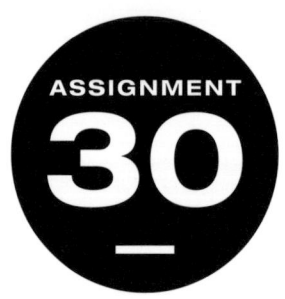

30

GALAXIES AND NEBULAE

Did you know that you can see some of the most interesting deep-sky objects (DSO) with nothing more than a camera? A DSO is any astronomical object that isn't a star or solar system object, so star clusters, nebulae, and galaxies. Most are so faint that they are invisible to the naked eye, but some are much brighter and are visible on dark, moonless nights.

Two of the easiest DSOs to see are the Andromeda Galaxy and the Orion Nebula. The Andromeda Galaxy, also called M31, is our closest neighboring galaxy and appears as a faint glowing cloud, while the Orion Nebula, also called M42, is a diffuse nebula in the Milky Way and looks like a fuzzy patch hanging below Orion's Belt. Your mission is to photograph one of these DSOs using advanced imaging techniques and specialist editing software.

Photographing a DSO is technically challenging and requires three types of "calibration" frames to be blended: lights, darks, and flats. Light frames capture the brightest details of a galaxy or nebula, dark frames are taken with the lens cap attached to the lens and are used to remove artefacts, and flat frames are perfectly white (fill the frame with a T-shirt or lightbox) and are designed to compensate for vignetting when merging your light and dark frames. Aim to shoot at least eight images of each type of "calibration" frame.

A telephoto lens with a minimum focal length of 200mm or a 20mm wideangle lens can be used for this assignment. Expose up for to 30 sec., set an ISO value of 1000, and select an aperture between f/2.8 and f/5.6. Longer integration will require a star tracker and accurate polar alignment (see Assignment 29).

TIPS

- A DSO shoot can take from 30 minutes to several hours, so make sure your spare batteries are fully charged, and you've got plenty of spare memory cards.

- Plan your DSO shoot to coincide with a new moon if possible and drive at least 20 minutes away from any towns or cities, so that light pollution is kept to an absolute minimum.

▶ *I captured this image of the Andromeda Galaxy (M31) and comet 12P/Pons–Brooks above a lone tree on the Mendip Hills using a five minute exposure.*

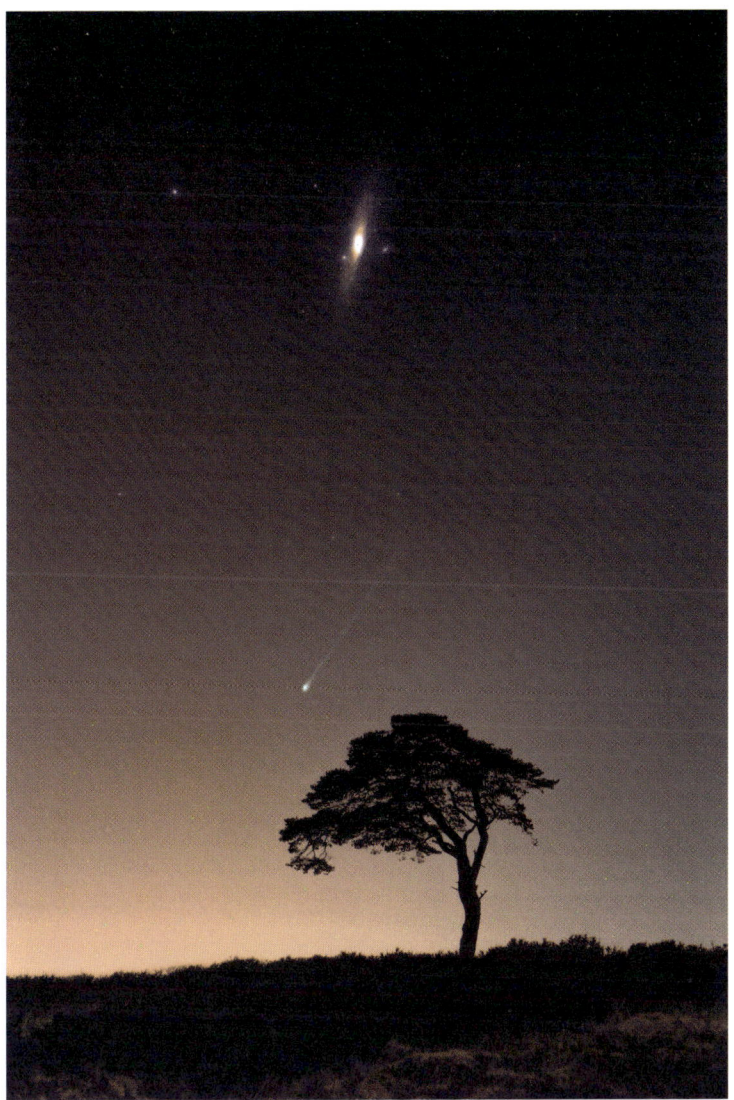

FIELD NOTES

The galaxies and nebulae we want to photograph can be thousands or millions of light-years away, and so the light from them can be very faint. Start with an ISO value of 1000 but don't be afraid to push it as far as you are comfortable with—the more images you can stack, even those taken at higher ISOs, the more detailed the final output will be.

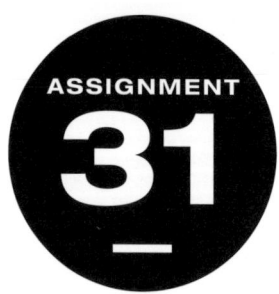

ASSIGNMENT
31

TIPS

- Timing is crucial for this assignment, so anticipate the moment when your subject is about to enter the frame.

- Painting with light is a trial-and-error technique. Assess your exposures and decide whether to let more or less light into your camera.

▶ *Long exposure can add a dynamic element to photographs at night. The light from car headlights puts a modern twist on the ancient landscape of Cheddar Gorge, and the scene is enhanced by the presence of the Milky Way and airglow.*

LONG EXPOSURES

Painting with light is a fun and creative technique that couples long exposures with a moving light source. When it comes to shooting nightscapes that include roads, an obvious source of moving lights is cars. For this assignment, find a scene that features a road and do your best to align this with a celestial subject such as a prominent constellation or the Milky Way. Wait until dark and start a long exposure when a car appears in the distance.

Position yourself a safe distance from the road, preferably from a high viewpoint, and pre-focus on your foreground. Use your widest lens or focal length, set an ISO of around 400, and start with a 10 sec. exposure. Timing is everything with this technique, so look out for a suitable light source and use a remote shutter release to trigger the shutter as soon as a car appears in the distance.

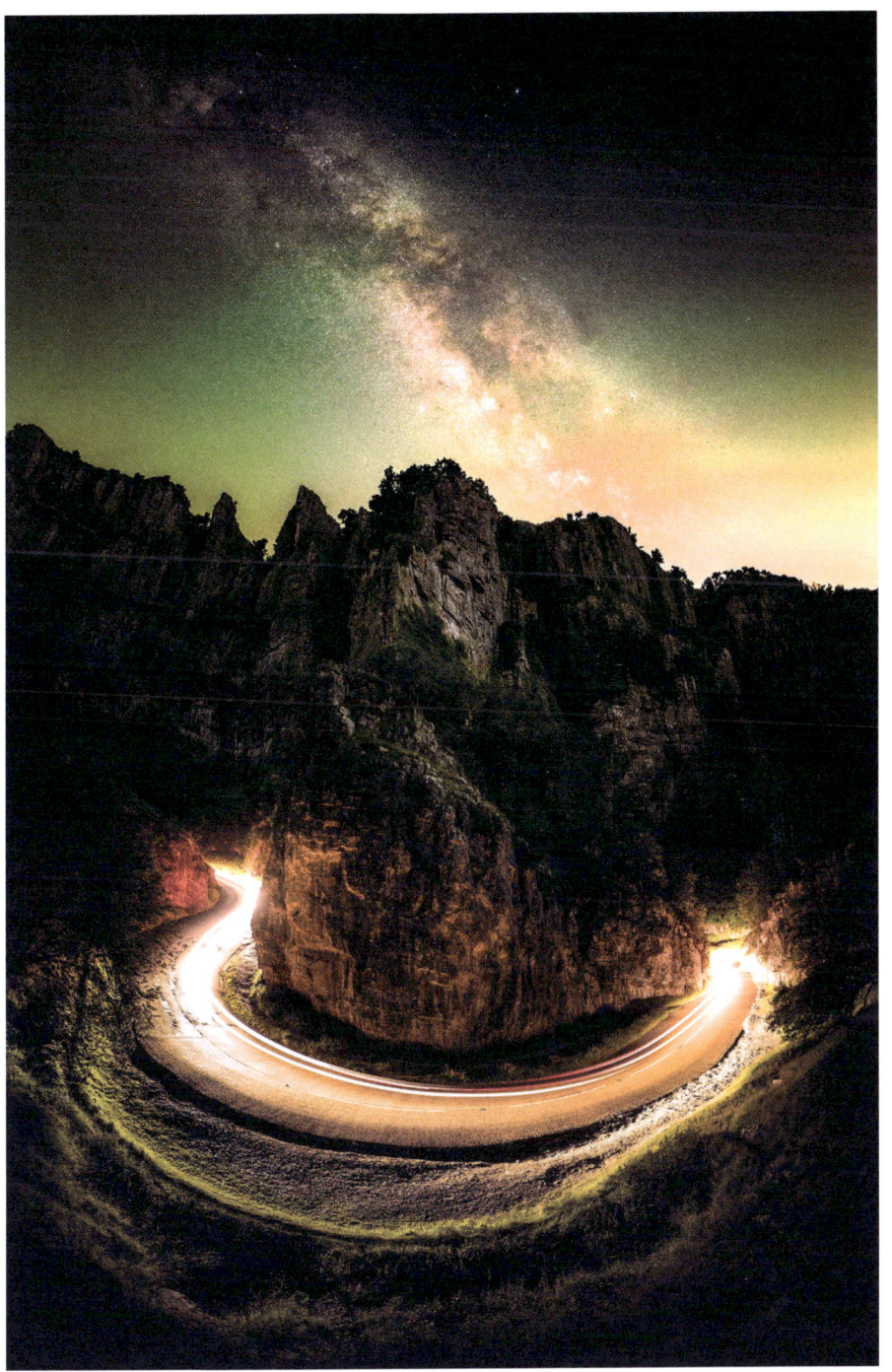

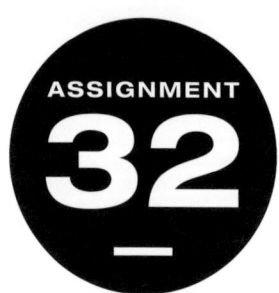

ASSIGNMENT
32

TIPS

- There are numerous specialist companies around the world that offer astro-modification services, including Spencer's Camera & Photo in the US and Infrared Camera Conversions in the UK.

- Shoot a series of light, dark, and flat frames as discussed in Assignment 30 to remove image artefacts and correct vignetting in your image.

▶ *Shooting long exposures of regions of space such as the Orion molecular complex captures a wealth of structure and detail. Astro-modified cameras let more of these wavelengths of light in.*

CAPTURE THE INVISIBLE

Some celestial structures are invisible to the unaided eye and can only be resolved using long exposures. For example, emission nebulae are clouds of ionized gas that emit their own light at optical wavelengths and can look spectacular when utilizing long exposures in excess of 30 sec. to capture these enormous structures.

The alternative is to convert a camera specifically for astrophotography. There are two types of astro-modification: hydrogen-alpha increase, which makes cameras four times more sensitive to H-alpha light; and full-spectrum modification, which replaces the internal infrared cut and ultraviolet filters with clear glass, making the camera sensitive to UV, visible, and infrared light. It should be noted that any form of modification will void your warranty, so consider this option carefully before astro-modifying your camera.

The aim of this assignment is to reveal the H-alpha light in the Orion molecular cloud complex. To do so, combine 10 "sub" shots, each exposed for 30sec., and "stretch" your image data by applying a series of Curves and Contrast adjustments.

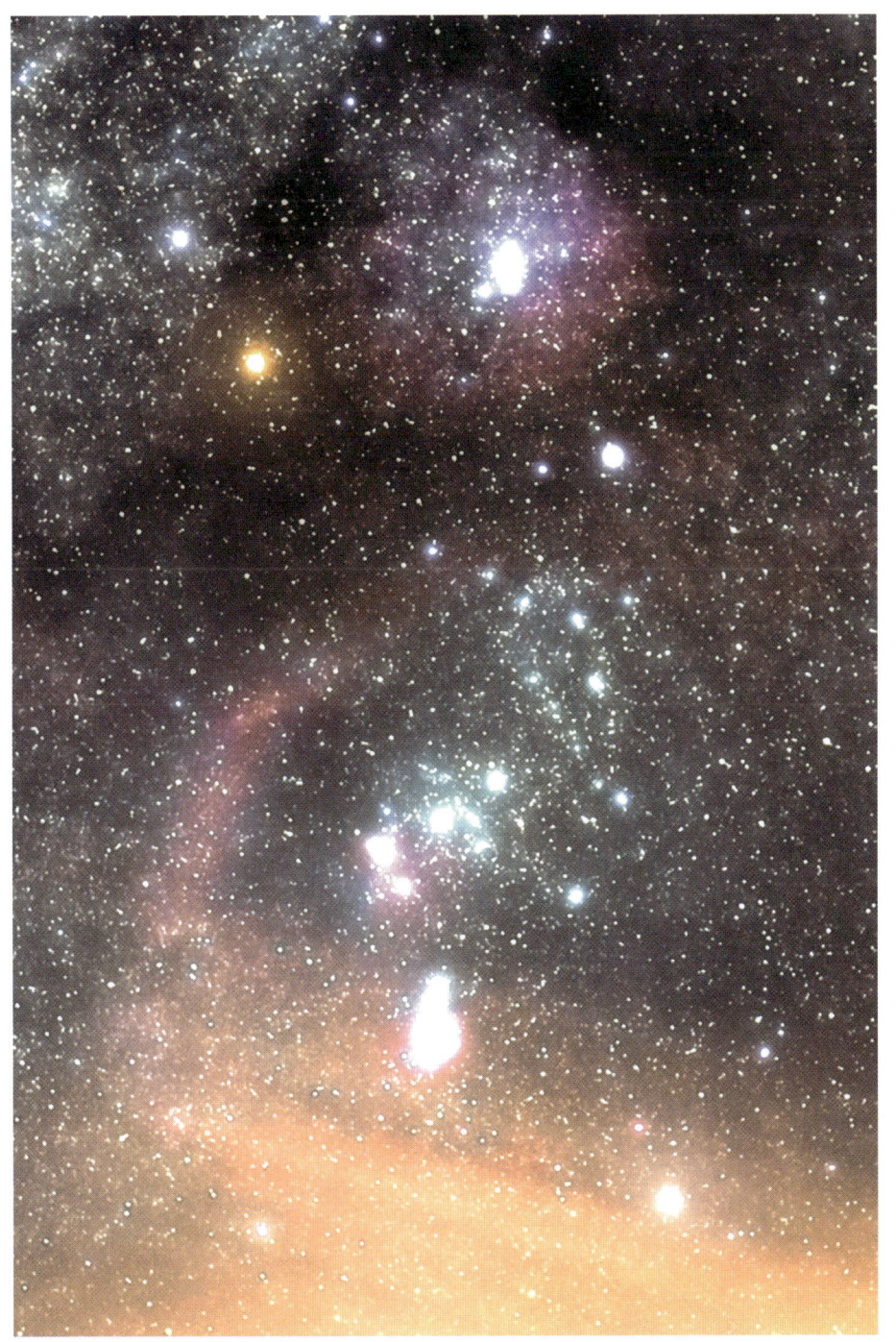

ASSIGNMENT 33

TIPS

• Shoot Raw files to preserve as much image detail as possible. This will also allow you to choose a higher-resolution video preset such as 4K or 8K.

• Presets such as HD may crop your original images, so you will need to select which areas of the frame to include in your time-lapse video clip.

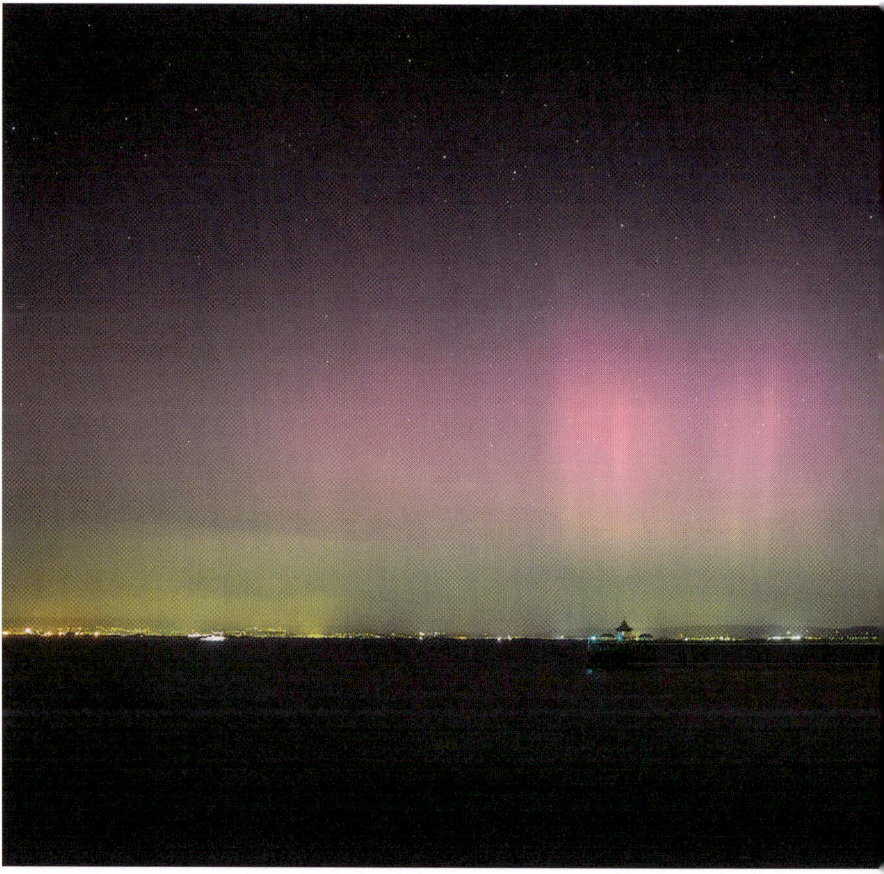

MOVING IMAGES

When you shoot a substantial number of images over a prolonged period, it's possible to turn these photos into a short time-lapse video using editing software such as Adobe Photoshop. Solar and lunar eclipses as well as star trails make for fascinating time-lapse videos. For this assignment, have a go at creating a short video clip of the dancing aurora (see Assignment 22).

To create a smooth time-lapse, you will need to shoot continuously for a minimum of 30 minutes. It takes 25 frames to create a single second of video footage, so use a preset of 25 frames per second (fps). Be sure to back up your images to a hard drive so you can import them directly to your editing software. Select your files, check the Sequence button, set your video presets (H2.64 1920x1080 resolution), and output your video clip.

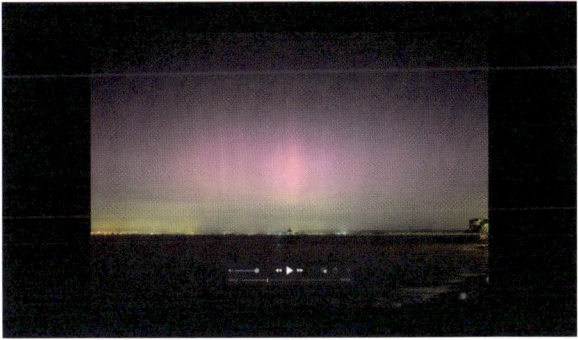

◀ *A still image from a time-lapse video clip of the northern lights above Clevedon Pier.*

ASSIGNMENT

34

TIPS

- Once you have successfully created a three-frame panorama, shoot a five- or seven-frame version. As your confidence grows, so too can your ambition.

- Try creating a vertical panorama. Start at your feet and keep shooting until your camera is pointing directly above your head.

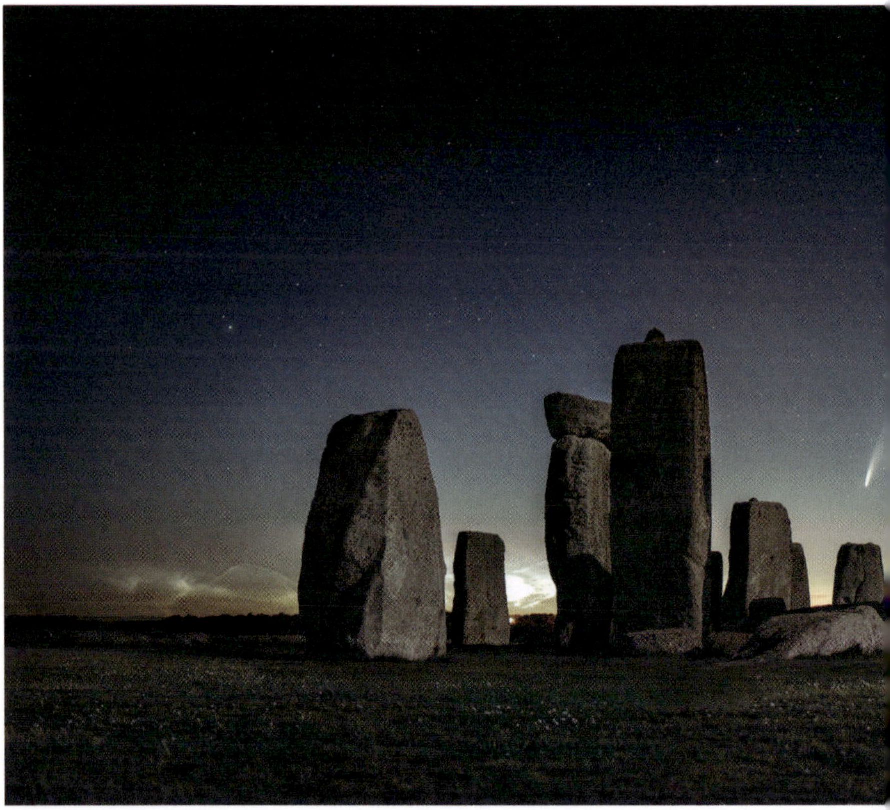

PANORAMAS

A panorama is a photograph with an ultra-wide field of view beyond that of a wideangle lens. These super-wide images are created by "stitching" several standard frames together. Your assignment is to create an epic "nightscape" panorama consisting of three frames.

Using your widest lens or focal length, overlap your three images by a third of the frame for a seamless "stitch." This requires precise framing, and a geared tripod head will help you to make more accurate adjustments. Shoot images up to a maximum of 30 sec. each to avoid star trailing in your images. Use a remote shutter release to minimize camera shake—sharp images are much easier to align in post-production.

▼ *Comet NEOWISE (C/2020 F3) above the iconic landmark that is Stonehenge.*

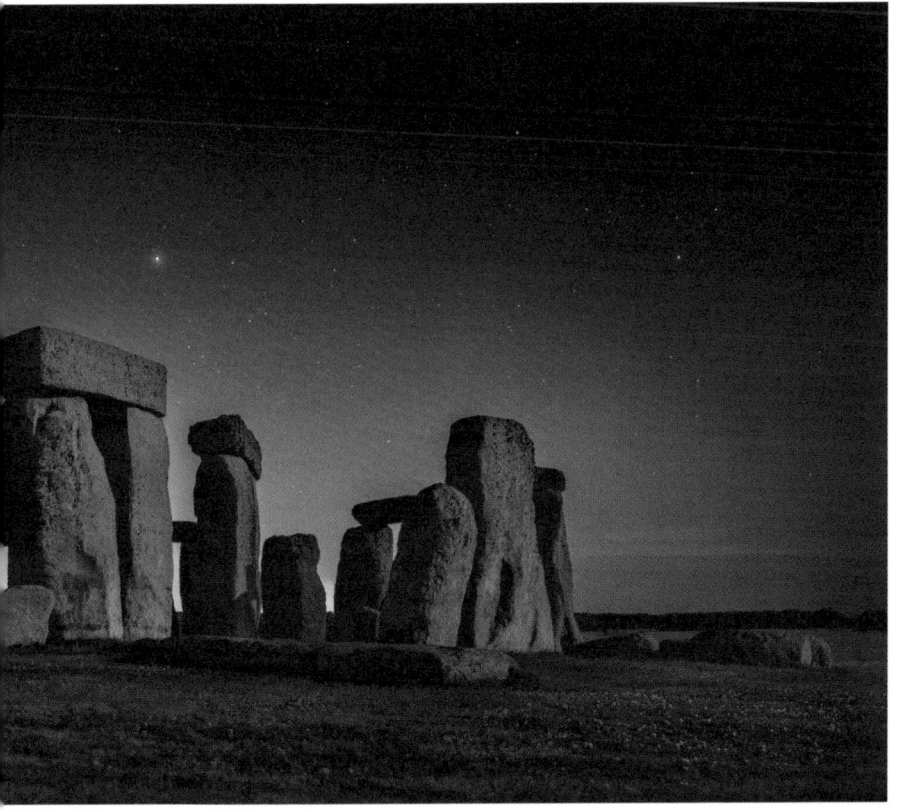

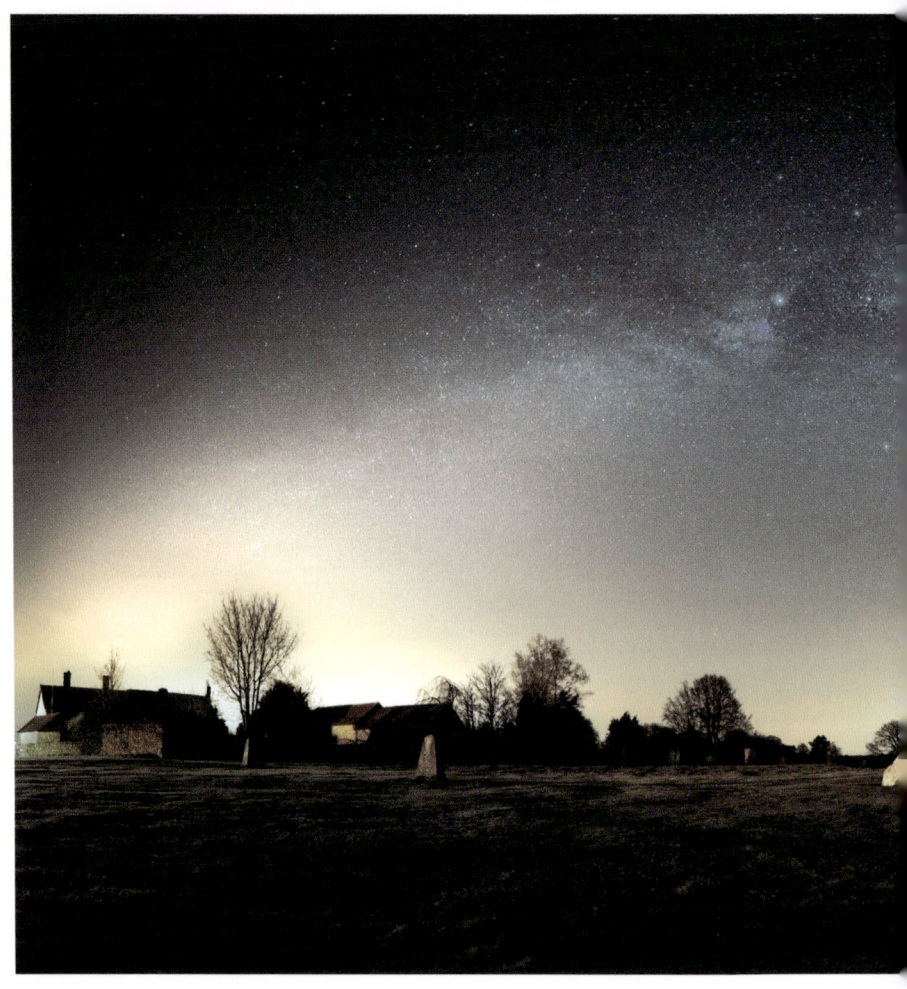

Adobe Photoshop and Lightroom feature powerful "merge" functions that automatically combine your selected files. Go to File > Automate > Photomerge (Photo > Photo Merge > Panorama Merge in Lightroom), select a layout and upload your files, and click OK. Your software will then seamlessly blend your three frames into one super-wide image.

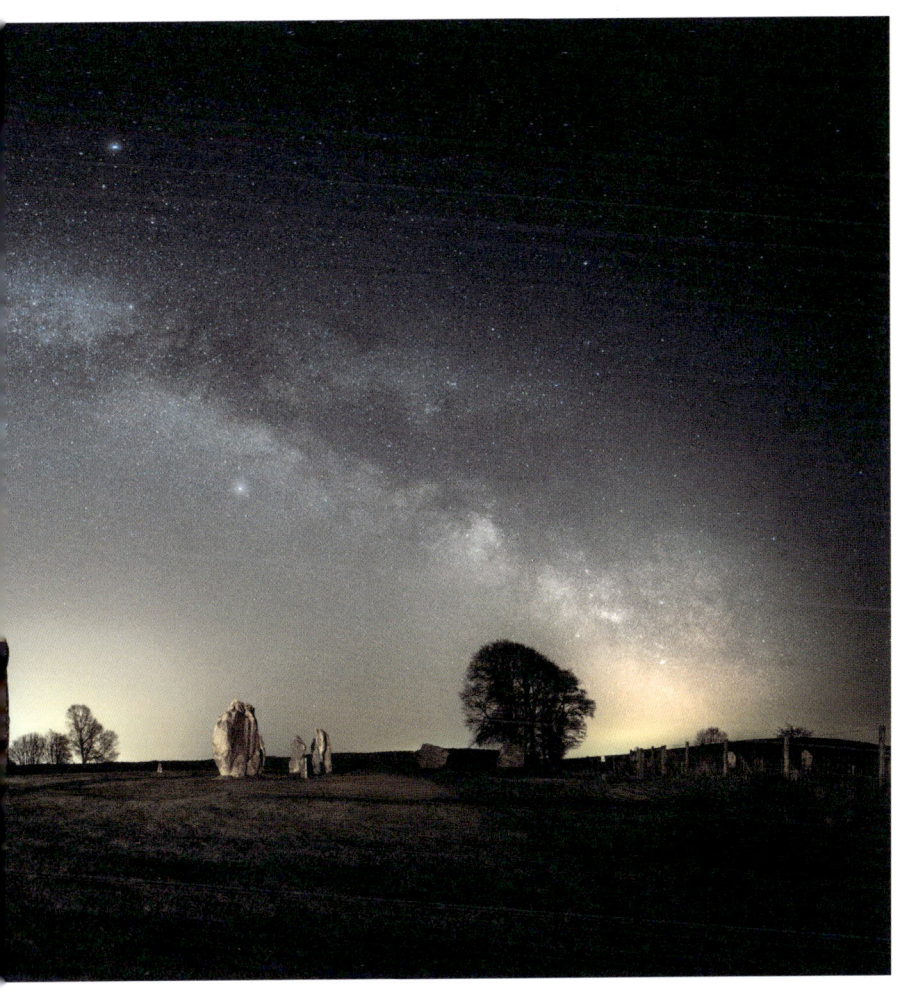

▲ *A panorama of the Milky Way galaxy stretching across the night sky above Avebury's stone circles.*

FIELD NOTES

To avoid vignetting, select an aperture of f/2.8 and adjust the shutter speed and ISO to balance the exposure. This will also help your photo-editing software to more easily stitch your images together.

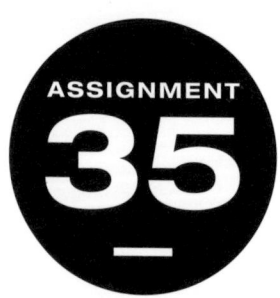

ASSIGNMENT

35

TIPS

- Consider the geographical orientation of your chosen location. For instance, you don't want to be looking south if you are observing the northern lights.

- What subject are you going to photograph? And what creative technique do you intend to use? These questions will help to resolve your narrative and map out your image.

LOCAL LANDSCAPES

As we will discover in Assignment 50, bucket-list locations tend to be very popular with photographers, but how often do you explore your local area in search of unique landscapes and stories? Not only can you visit your local area repeatedly and become more familiar with your surroundings, but you also cut down on the need to travel far to create unique images.

This assignment is all about using your local knowledge to locate and photograph distinct subject matter. Resources such as Google Maps and Pixeo will help you find natural formations, local landmarks, and viewpoints within a 20-mile radius of where you live, and visit museums and talk to locals to find out more about your area's history.

If you live in a large town or city, you will need to travel 10 miles or so to minimize the effects of light pollution. Ideal night-sky subjects include the Milky Way (see Assignment 13) and the classic winter constellations Orion, Taurus, and Gemini (see Assignment 14). Use local landmarks to emphasize the "local" part of the assignment and mix and match techniques to test your creativity.

FIELD NOTES

Taking photographs of local landscapes is a great way to explore your story as a photographer. Is there a subject that hasn't been photographed before or could be photographed in a different way? Look through the remaining assignments and see if there are combinations that you feel could work well for your images.

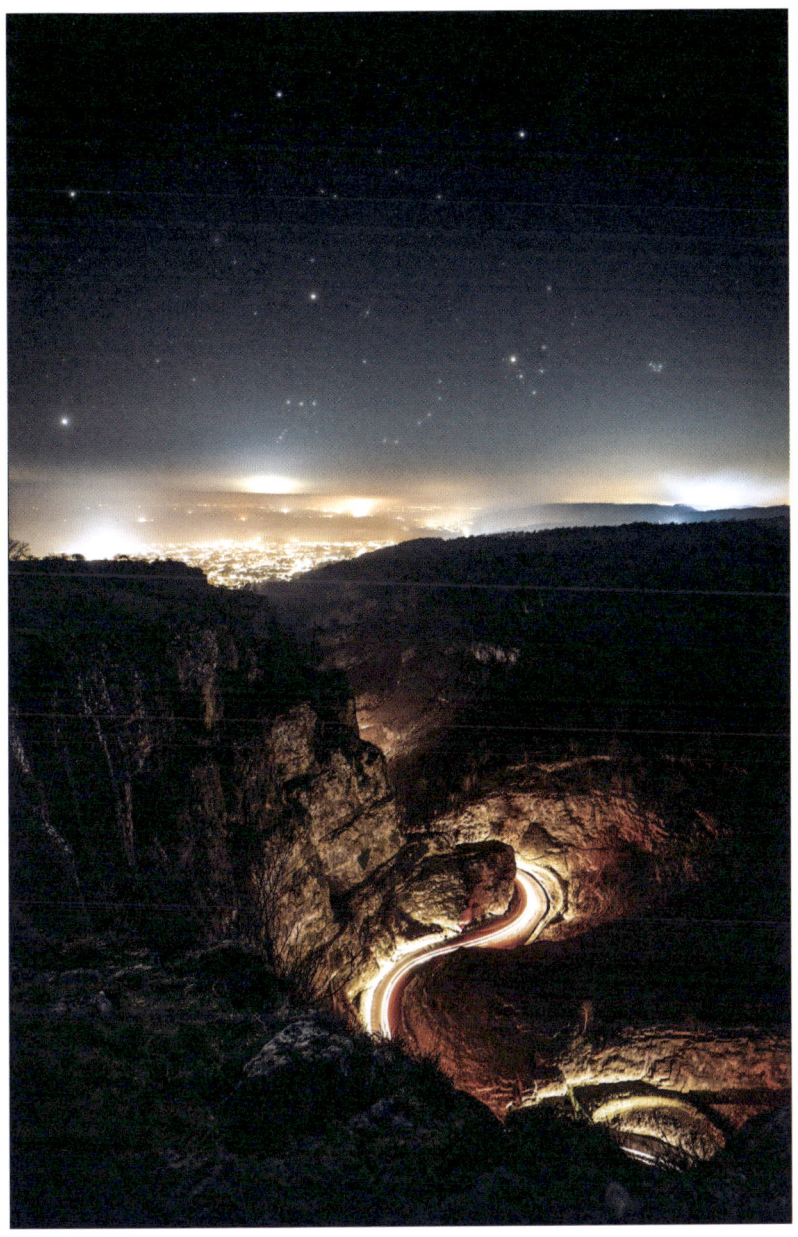

▲ *I used online maps to locate a safe viewpoint to capture the winter constellations setting above Horseshoe Bend at Cheddar Gorge.*

ASSIGNMENT

36

TIPS

- Learn to identify the brighter stars and constellations, as these will be the most visible, even in areas of strong light pollution.

- Try to avoid shooting in the center of large cities and towns, as the light pollution will be too intense.

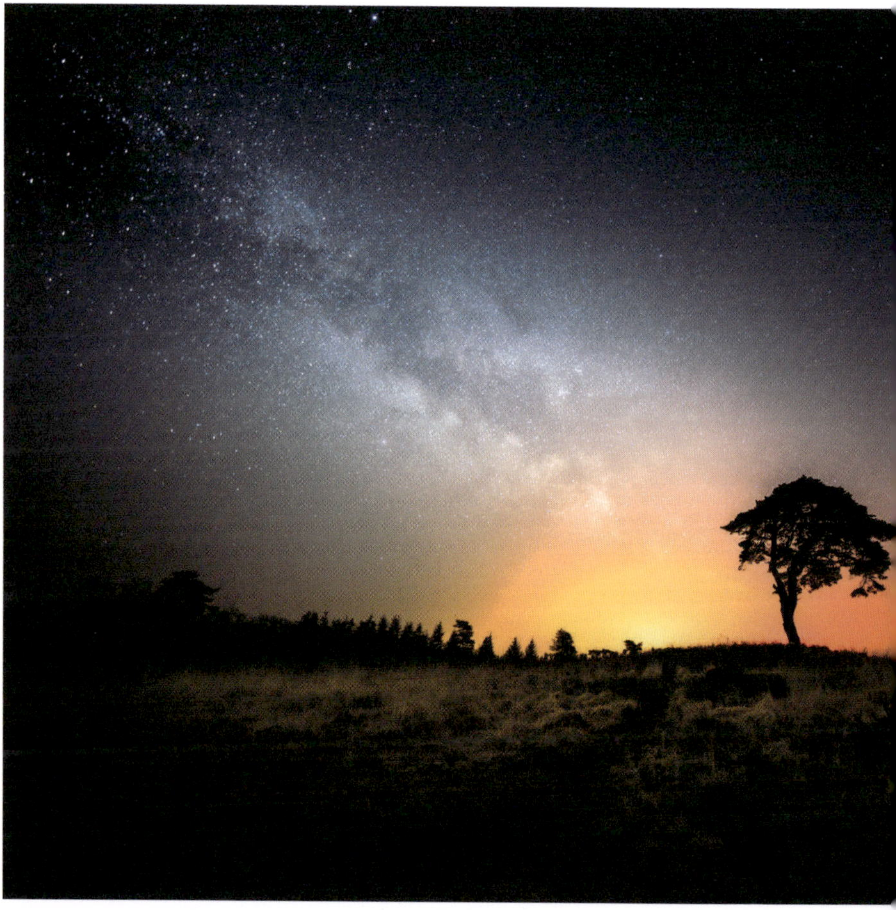

LIGHT-POLLUTED LANDSCAPES

You don't always need to travel to dark-sky locations to appreciate the stars, as it is still possible to take incredible night images from light-polluted areas. The only problem with shooting near large towns and cities is that light pollution severely reduces the contrast of the stars and so only those with a greater surface brightness (or magnitude) will be visible. The purpose of this assignment is to encourage those of you who aren't able to travel out of light-polluted areas to photograph the stars as best as you can.

One accessory you may find invaluable for this assignment is a natural-night filter. These glass filters minimize the effects of light pollution by cutting the frequencies of artificial lighting and are available in a wide range of sizes.

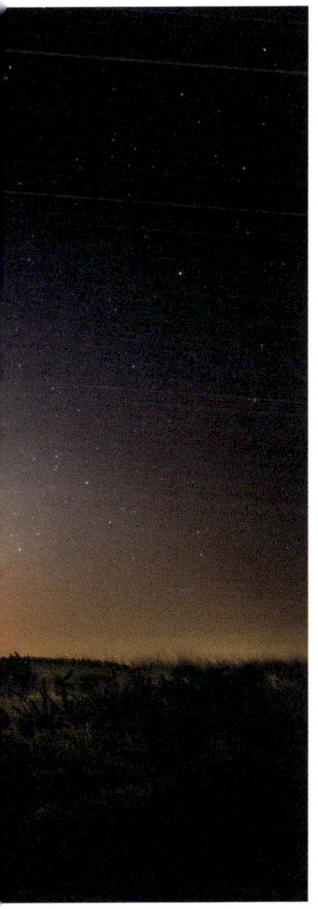

As there will be more artificial light in the scene, expect exposures to be much shorter—shutter speeds of just a few seconds are needed to identify the major constellations. An aperture of f/4 and an ISO of between 100 and 200 are ideal, although you may need to adjust these settings depending on location. The use of a natural-night filter will boost the contrast between the stars and your foreground.

◄ *Light-polluted landscapes not only provide a vibrant color palette, they also tell a story of our changing environment and the increasing threat to dark skies. This scene captures a lone tree and the rising Milky Way silhouetted by the light pollution from a nearby city.*

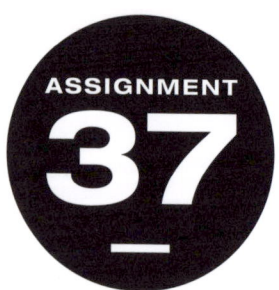

ASSIGNMENT 37

TIPS

- Set up your equipment in advance so you are prepared for a night under the stars. Attaching your tripod plate to your camera, for instance, can save time.

- Reduce the brightness of your camera's LCD screen so it won't greatly affect your night vision. This control is typically found in your camera's settings menu.

▼ *The Bortle dark-sky index measured on a scale of 1 to 9, with 1 indicating dark skies and 9 identifying severely light-polluted areas.*

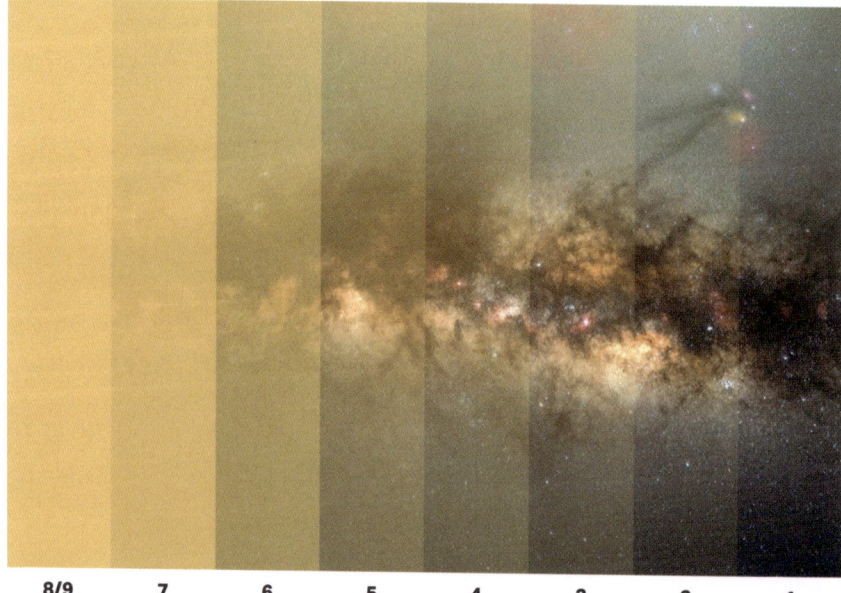

8/9	7	6	5	4	3	2	1
City/inner city sky	City/ suburban transition	Bright suburban sky	Suburban sky	Suburban/ rural transition	Rural sky	Dark-sky site	Excellent dark-sky site

DARK-SKY SITES

A dark-sky site is an area that isn't adversely affected by artificial light at night (ALAN). These sites provide us with a window to the universe and, if you've never visited one before, can be positively overwhelming. The night sky's brightness is measured by the Bortle scale, with Class 1 being the darkest and Class 9 being the brightest. True dark-sky sites are Class 1 and should be treated with the utmost respect, as not only are they often rich in wildlife, but the use of artificial light is often prohibited by law.

For this assignment, you will need to use your resources to locate a Class 1 location and plan and shoot a night-sky image with little to no artificial light sources. Use the widest focal length you have at your disposal to capture the maximum amount of light and detail, and fill the top two-thirds of your frame with the sky and the bottom third with your foreground. This will help you to fully appreciate the immensity of a truly dark sky unaffected by light pollution.

To locate Class 1 locations, use an app called Light Pollution Map. This free app is available for both Apple and Android phones and provides a color-coded map overlay, with Class 1 areas highlighted in dark blue. I highly recommend you download it.

Because the contrast between sky and stars will be noticeably more pronounced, clarity will be greater and shutter speeds will generally be shorter, although subtler details in the night sky can be revealed with longer shutter speeds. Experiment with exposure settings and compare results to see which approach you prefer.

FIELD NOTES

Bortle Class 1 locations are very dark and so extra care must be taken with regard to your environment and the wildlife around you. Your eyes take 20-30 minutes to fully adapt to the dark, and artificial light can hinder this process, which is why a red flashlight is essential when moving around and setting up your camera.

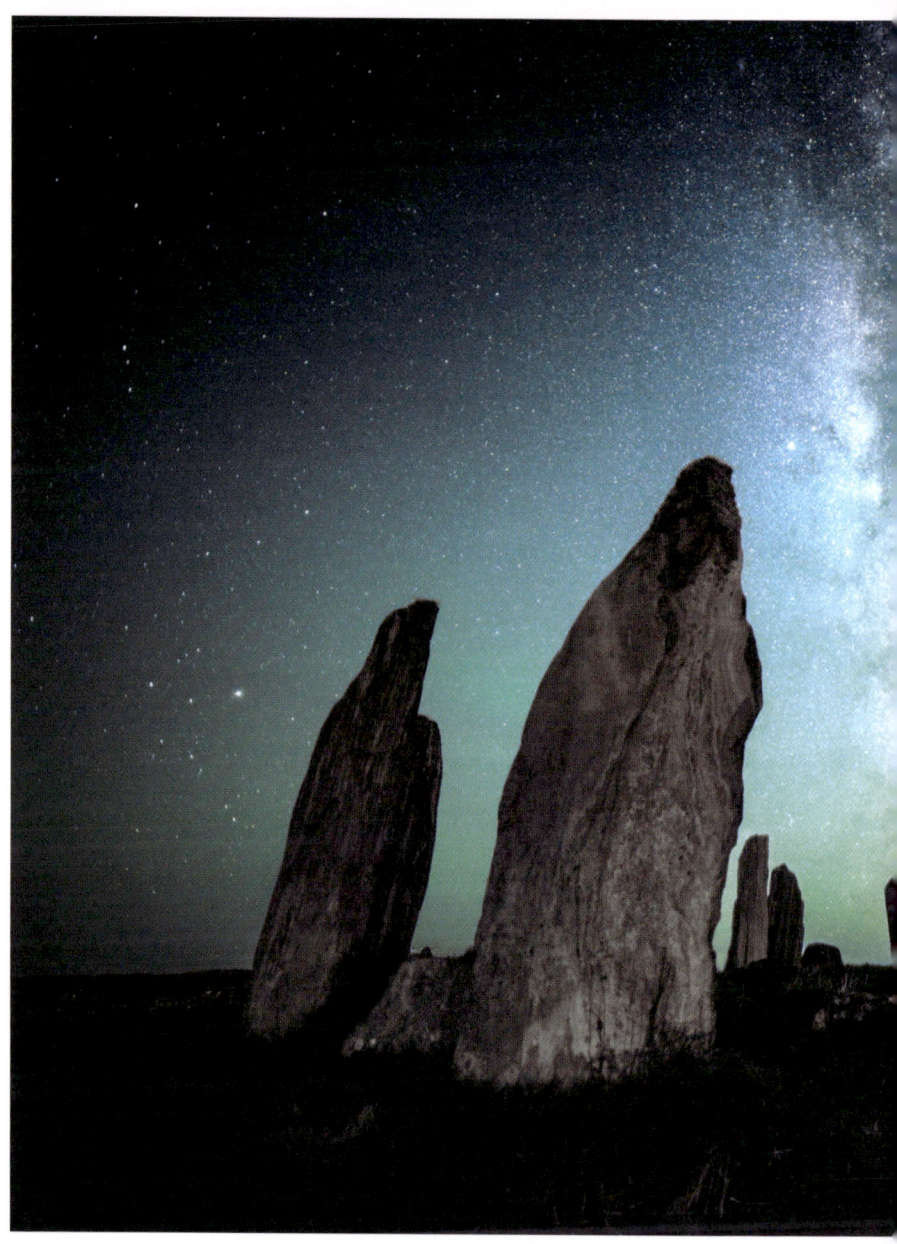

▲ *My first experience of a Bortle Class 1 location was at the Callanish Stones on the Isle of Lewis. I experimented with exposure settings and will never forget the moment when this image first appeared on my camera's rear LCD screen—I was mesmerized by the detail in the arms of the Milky Way.*

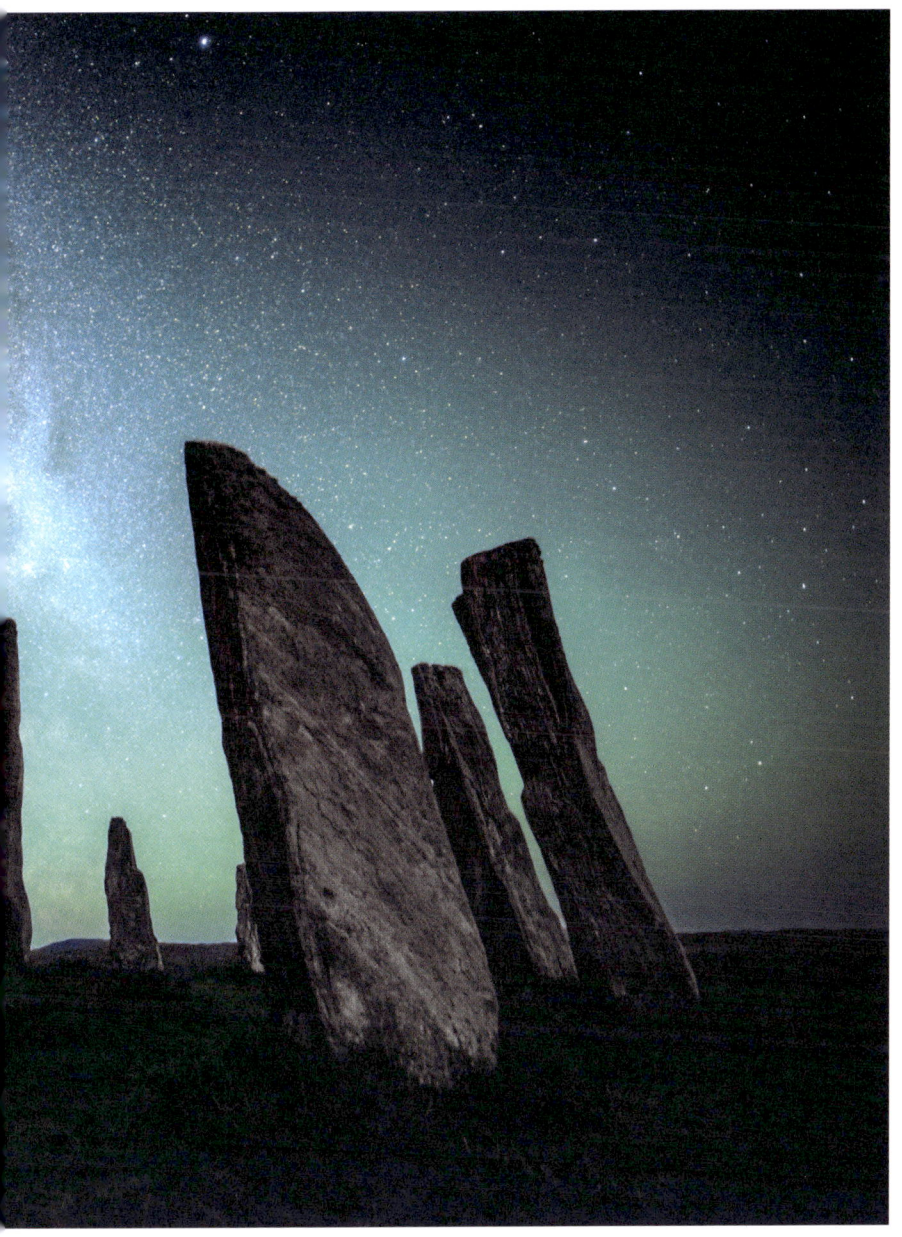

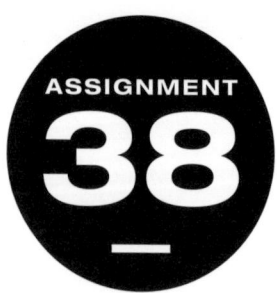

ASSIGNMENT
38

TIPS

- Observatories are private properties, so unless you have obtained permission in advance, never trespass.

- Different techniques can be used to tell different stories. For instance, star trails capture the passing of time. See Assignment 17 for more on star trails.

▶ *The Milky Way captured from the Mullard Radio Astronomy Observatory in Cambridge.*

OBSERVATORIES

Are we alone in our universe? This question has obsessed scientists for centuries—and we still don't have a definitive answer. But that doesn't stop professional observatories around the world from translating wavelengths of light from distant stars to better understand the universe and its evolution. For this assignment, take a photograph juxtaposing an observatory with a celestial body.

For reasons of security, observatories aren't always the most accessible of places, but it's often possible to find nearby roads or footpaths to shoot from using online maps. For instance, Google Maps' Street View mode is a great way to scout locations, plan compositions, and get a sense of what might be visible at night.

For images of observatories and the Milky Way, it's important to contextualize the subject matter and emphasize the vastness of the night sky compared to the size of the observatories, so a wide to mid-range focal length between 20mm and 50mm will work best. Select the widest aperture your lens allows, set ISO to around 640, and aim for a shutter speed of 5–10 sec. Your final image should capture foreground details with the stars clearly visible.

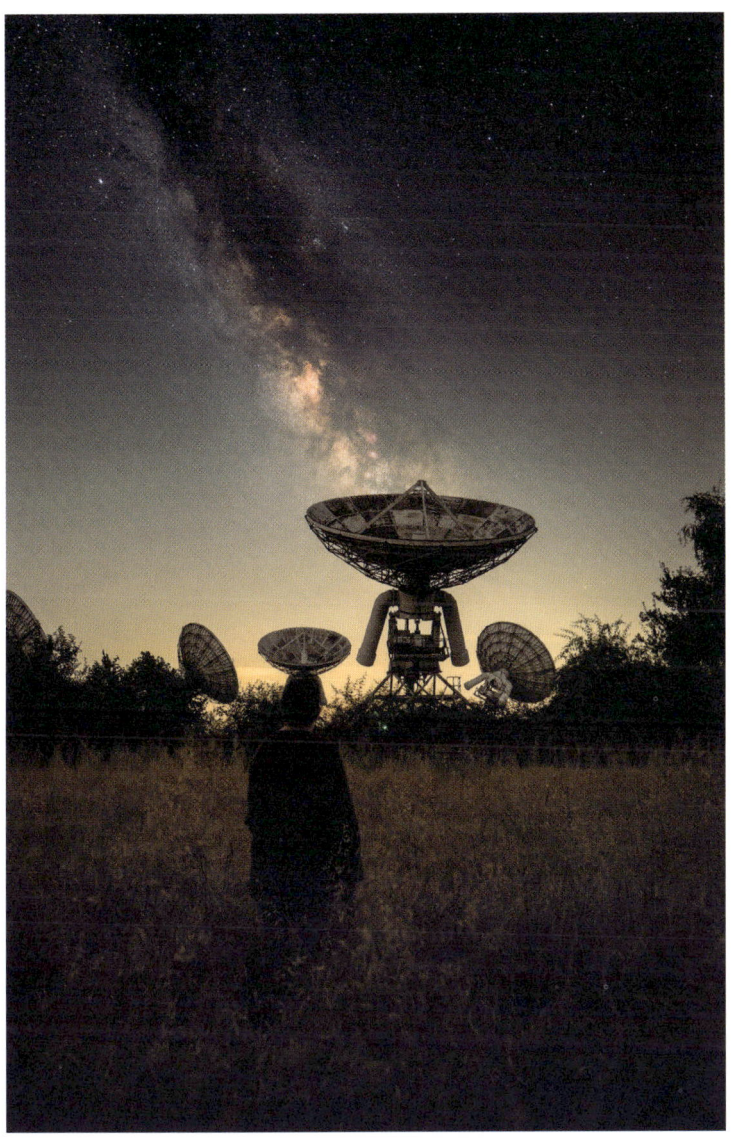

FIELD NOTES

Be aware that observatories can make loud noises as the telescopes and satellite dishes move. This caught me out the first time I visited one at night, but once I became more aware of my surroundings, the atmosphere added to the experience.

ASSIGNMENT
39

TIPS

- ISS tracker websites and apps use Coordinated Universal Time (UTC), so make sure you allow for any +/- time differences.

- Although clear skies are preferable, some cloud obstruction can add an extra layer of interest to your ISS photographs, so don't be put off by adverse weather conditions.

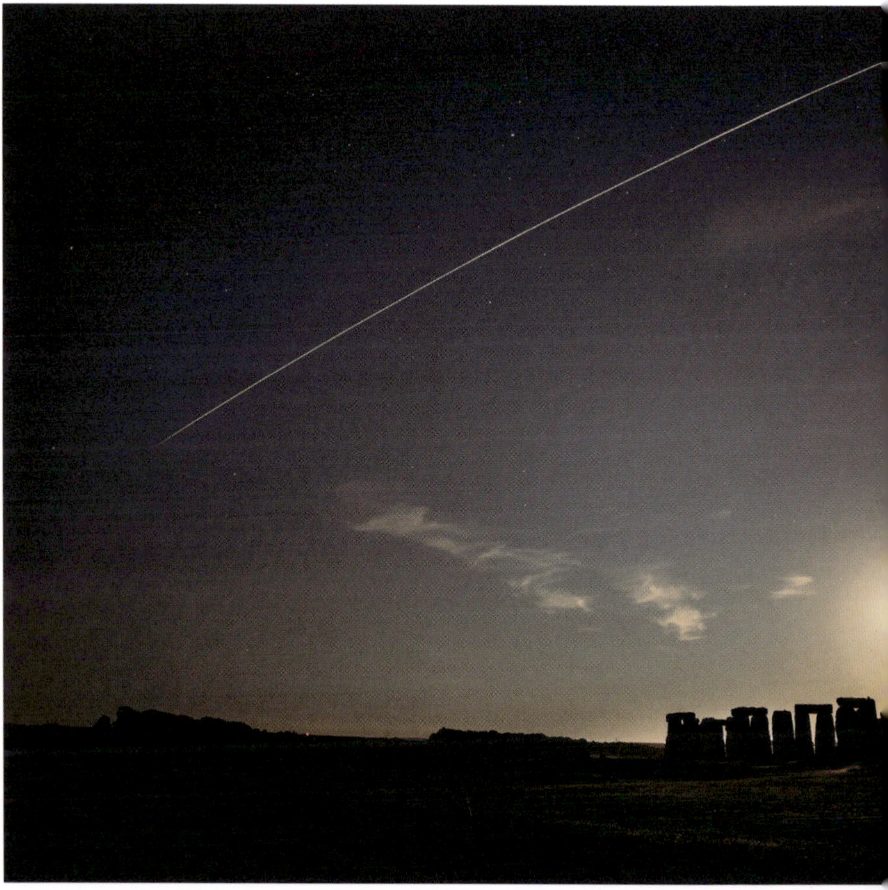

INTERNATIONAL SPACE STATION

The International Space Station (ISS) has been orbiting Earth for over 25 years and is visible to the naked eye if you know where and when to look up. It's one of the brightest objects in the night sky and looks like a fast-moving airplane. There are numerous websites and apps dedicated to tracking the ISS—my favorite is www.heavens-above.com, which includes an interactive ISS "visualization" feature.

Your challenge here is to photograph a pass of the ISS above a subject of interest. Because the ISS can take several seconds to pass overhead, you may need to push your shutter speed up to 10 sec. You then need to consider your remaining camera settings, keeping ISO levels low to minimize the adverse effects of noise. On this occasion, you may also need to stop down (reduce the physical size of the aperture) to let less light into the camera.

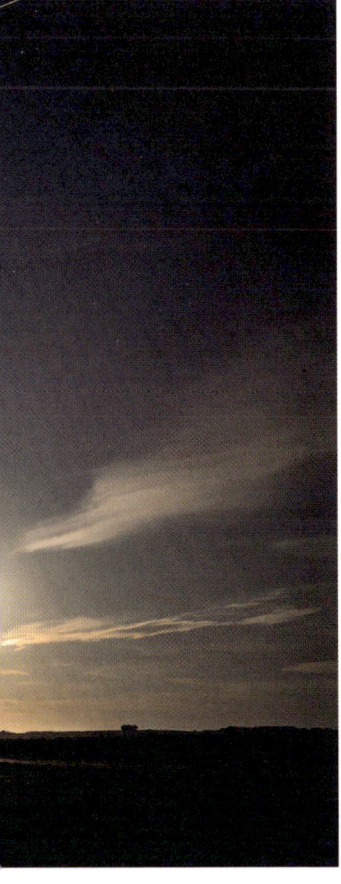

You also need to consider the effects of Earth's rotation. Instead of shooting a single exposure, take a series of continuous exposures and "stack" them at the editing stage. This will keep the stars in your final image sharp.

◀ *The International Space Station flies over Stonehenge—two incredible feats of human engineering.*

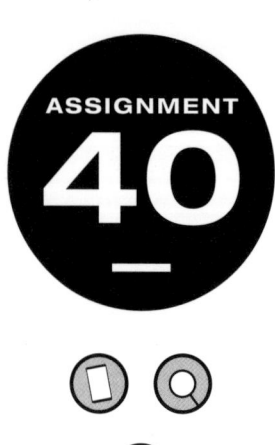

ASSIGNMENT
40
—

TIPS

- Satellites appear close together shortly after deployment—this is known as a "satellite train." They eventually spread out as their elevation increases.

- Satellites in low Earth orbit appear to move very fast, so limit your exposure times to no more than 10 sec.

- Watching a group of 60 or so satellites passing overhead can be an overwhelming experience, so brace yourself if you haven't seen a satellite train before.

MEGA-CONSTELLATIONS

In addition to the impact of light pollution, we are now seeing the emergence of "mega-constellations"—groups of satellites being launched into low Earth orbit (LEO) to provide global internet coverage. Although these mega-constellations improve global communications, the vast number of satellites could soon outnumber the visible stars, potentially changing our view of the night sky forever.

There are several resources you can use to plan satellite passes and determine how many satellites will be visible. A good app to use is See a Satellite Tonight by James Darpinian. This is available as both an app (Android only) and an online resource (james.darpinian.com/satellites) and uses your GPS location to predict exact times and brightness of a satellite pass. Check the weather and look for clear skies.

As with the International Space Station (see Assignment 39), longer exposures of around 10 sec. will typically lead to stronger images. Keep your aperture as wide as your lens allows and set ISO to 400 to retain detail, then switch your camera's shooting mode to Continuous. When the satellites appear, use your remote shutter release to shoot a minimum of 20 images. When editing your images, "stack" these frames to create a single image that shows the satellites as a continuous streak across the night sky.

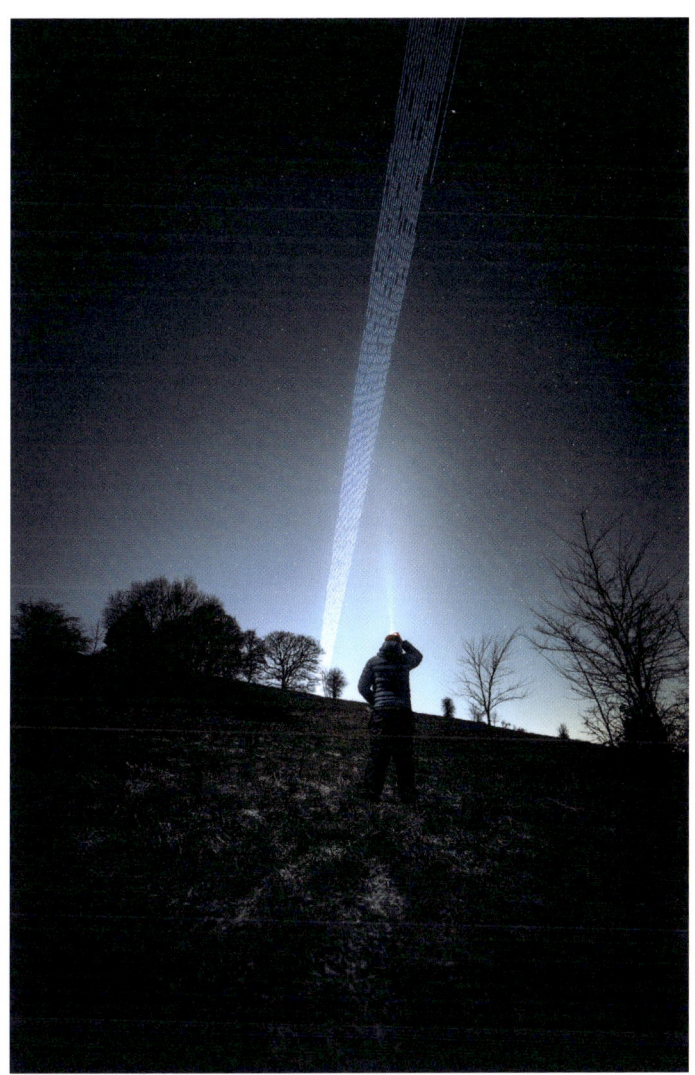

▲ *This image captures the early stages of a satellite train as it passes. Looking west, I waited for the first satellites to emerge over the horizon. I was then able to "stack" a series of long exposures to create my final output.*

FIELD NOTES

Any form of satellite moves very fast through the frame, but what makes mega-constellations more apparent is the sheer quantity. They are most visible just before dawn or just after dusk, as they reflect light from the sun.

ASSIGNMENT

41

TIPS

- New subject matter will push you out of your comfort zone, but it will also build your confidence, so embrace the challenge and see where the story takes you.

- Whatever technique you use for this assignment, don't forget the basics of night photography: weather, light pollution, and appropriate kit.

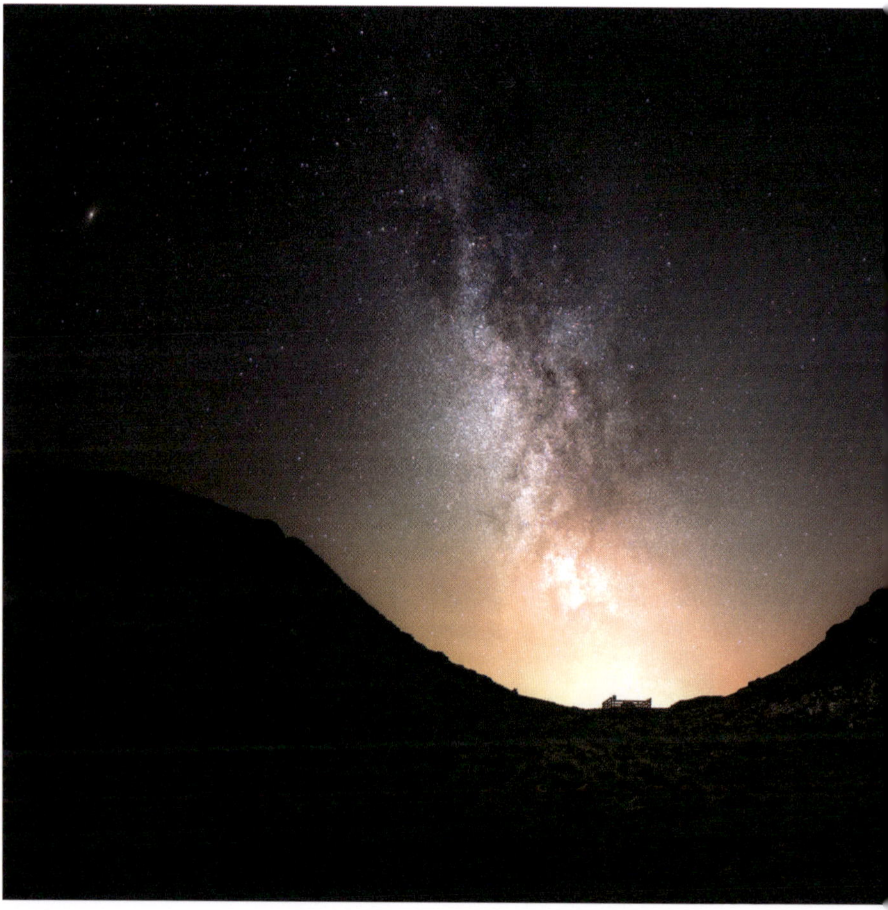

CHANGES IN THE LANDSCAPE

Photography rarely makes headlines, but when it does, it's often in relation to the importance of our national landmarks. One such example was the felling of the Sycamore Gap tree in Northumberland, England, in September 2023. This incredibly sad news sent shockwaves throughout the photographic community and was rightly labeled an act of senseless vandalism.

Your challenge is to create a photograph at night that brings a newsworthy story to life. Start by researching newspapers and websites in search of stories that relate to the night sky and celestial events, then think about which photographic techniques you could use to help tell the story.

When visualizing your newsworthy compositions, ask yourself these questions: What is the story? What do I want to say? How do I want to tell it? Perhaps even write a headline for your image. The clearer your artistic vision, the easier it will be to choose a suitable technique and tell your story.

◀ *The light of the Milky Way shines down onto the landscape at Sycamore Gap, filling the space and illuminating the roots of this famous tree.*

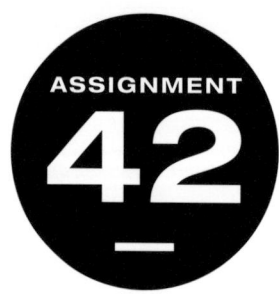

TIPS

- The rule of thirds can be used in both landscape and portrait orientations, so don't be afraid to rotate the camera if you want to add more vertical interest.

- If you want to place greater visual emphasis on the area of land immediately in front of your camera, compose a scene comprising one-third sky and two-thirds foreground.

▶ *This composition demonstrates that filling the frame with a ratio of two-thirds sky to one-third foreground can help to draw the viewer into the scene.*

THE RULE OF THIRDS

The rule of thirds is a powerful composition guideline designed to create visual balance. By dividing your frame into nine equally sized rectangles using vertical and horizontal lines, you end up with a 3x3 grid and two intersecting crosshairs or "power points." If you position key pictorial elements such as horizons along the grid lines, and focal points on the power points, you create stronger compositions.

For this assignment, use the rule of thirds to compose a well-balanced nightscape. Start by activating your camera's 3x3 overlay, which superimposes the rule-of-thirds grid over the rear LCD screen or electronic viewfinder (EVF), then use the overlay to compose a scene comprising two-thirds sky and one-third foreground. Take a second shot with the horizon running through the center of the frame and compare the results. Which composition creates a greater sense of visual balance?

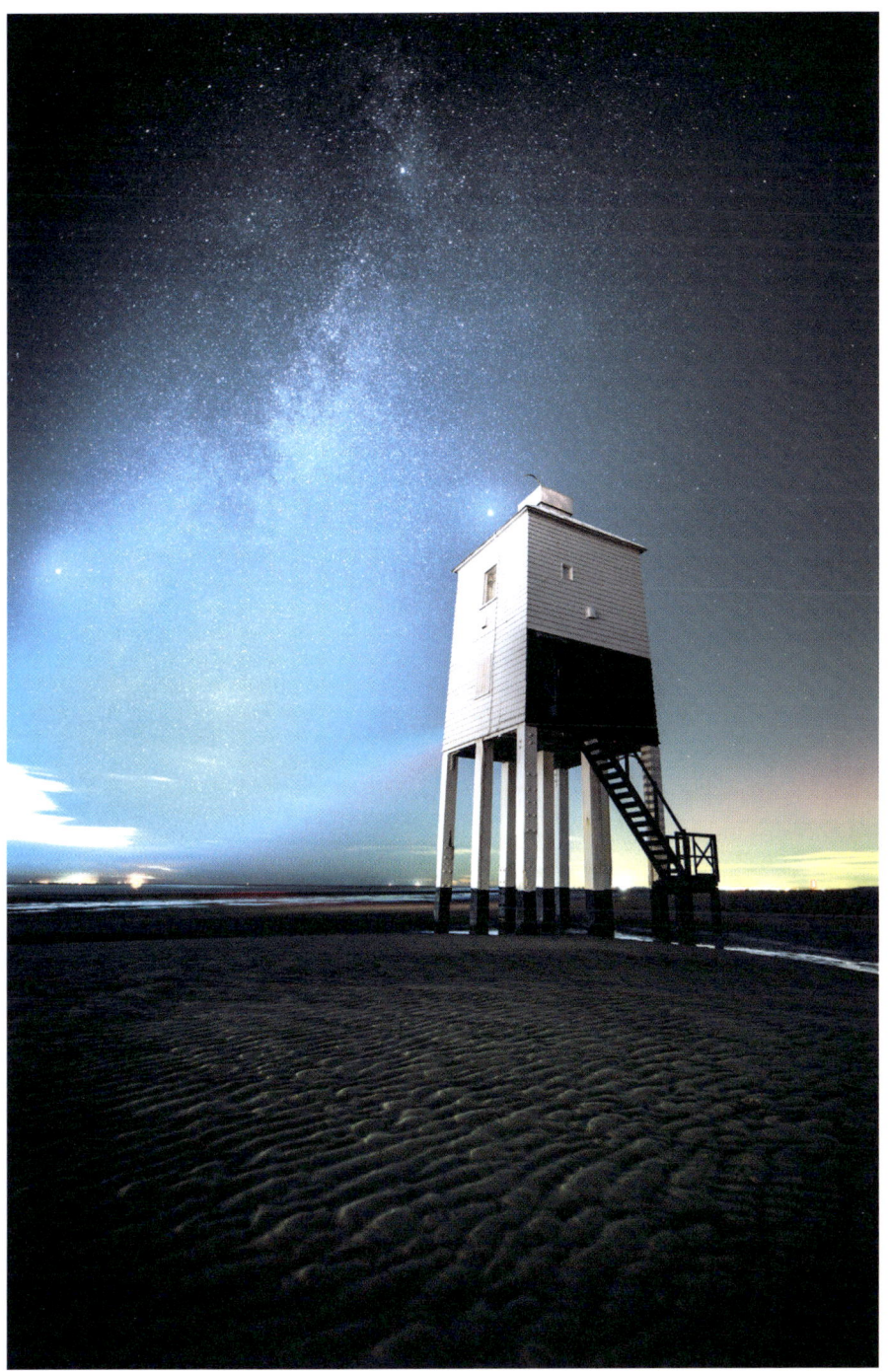

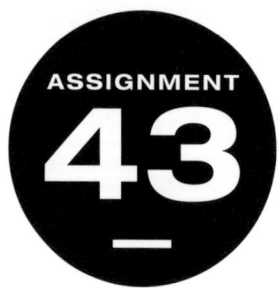

ASSIGNMENT
43

TIPS

• Start by positioning your leading line in a lower corner of the frame to draw the viewer's eye into the scene.

• Use a wideangle lens to exaggerate and distort the angles of leading lines closest to the camera.

▶ *The houses on either side of Gold Hill in Shaftesbury create leading lines into the center of the frame, with the Milky Way above.*

LEADING LINES

Leading lines are compositional devices used to create a sense of depth and to guide the viewer's eye from one part of a scene to another. These lines often start at the bottom of the frame and guide the eye upward, although diagonal lines can also be used to great effect. Leading lines can be natural or artificial, from roads and rivers to rocks on a beach, and are often deployed to draw attention to a particular subject or focal point.

Converging lines are lines that appear to get closer to each other as they recede. The point at which converging lines meet is known as the "vanishing point." The inclusion of converging lines and vanishing points is a great way to enhance the illusion of depth and can be exaggerated by shooting from higher viewpoints.

For this assignment, shoot a portrait-orientated nightscape that incorporates a strong example of a leading line. Look for a foreground subject that instinctively makes you want to explore the scene and experiment with high and low viewpoints. Think about where the leading line takes the viewer—you want to lead the eye toward a point of interest rather than out of the frame.

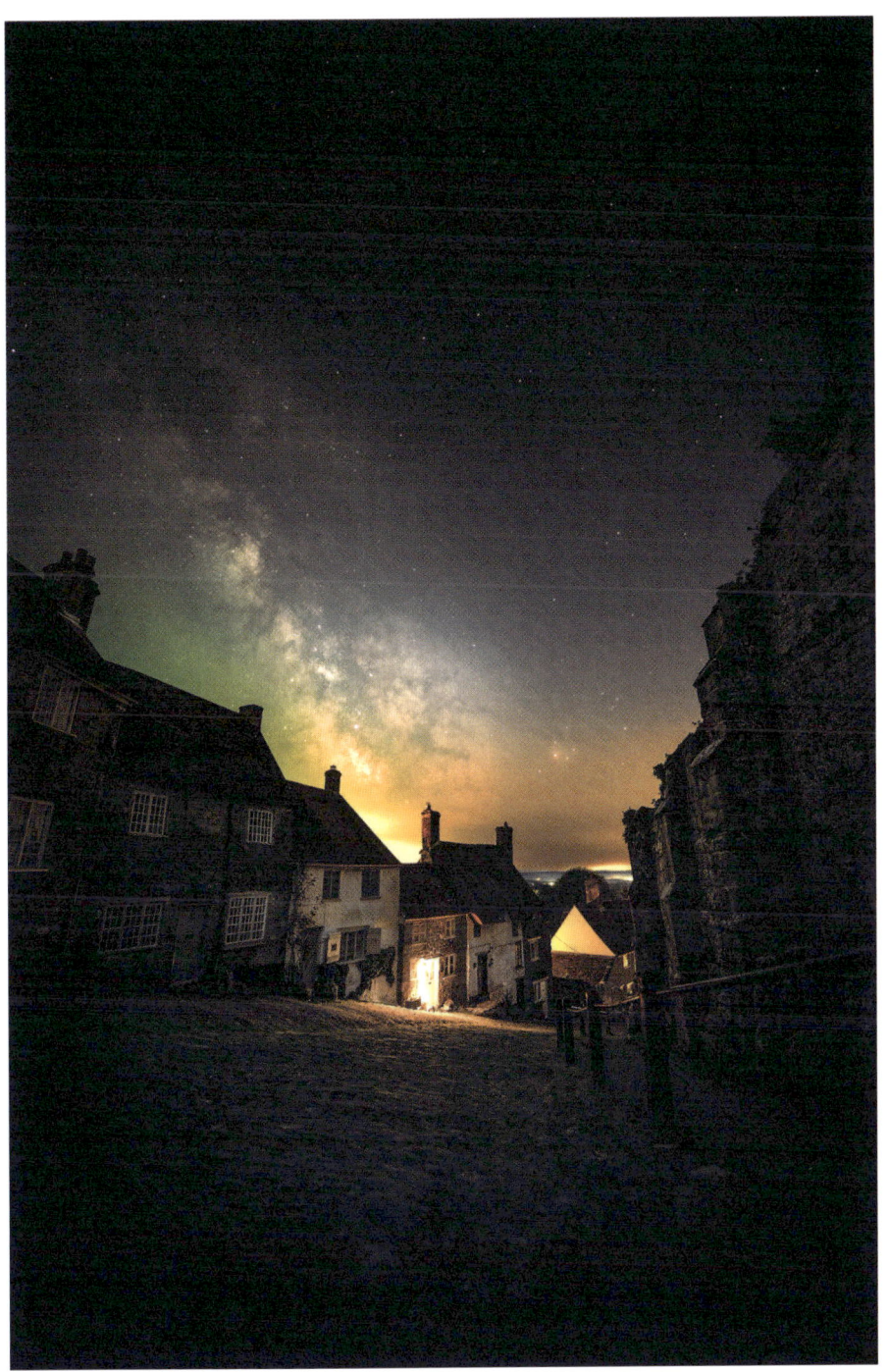

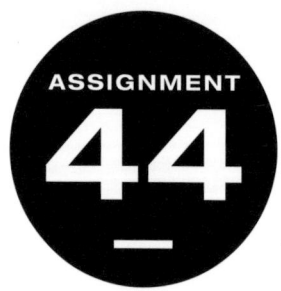

ASSIGNMENT
44

TIPS

• Extend your tripod to its maximum height and point your camera down slightly to include more of your immediate foreground. This will exaggerate the wideangle effect.

• Wider focal lengths can be used to exaggerate and emphasize foreground scale, while longer focal lengths can be used to condense perspective.

▶ *The slope of the foreground rock face in this image of Llanddwyn Bay invites the viewer into the scene, drawing our eye along the winding path up to the lighthouse.*

TO THE FORE

Composition is all about how we arrange the visual elements within the frame to influence how the viewer's eye is directed through a photograph. Color, contrast, lines, curves, shapes, patterns, textures, symmetry, asymmetry, negative space, sharpness, and blur are all important elements of composition that help us choreograph our story. Three-dimensional scenes can also be divided into foreground, midground, and background zones. For this assignment, we're going to be focusing on foregrounds.

Getting close to a foreground subject and shooting with a wideangle lens to exaggerate perspective is a great way to add impact and create a sense of depth. The only caveat for night photography is that we may need to "stack" several images to ensure front-to-back sharpness since most lenses are at their sharpest at mid-range apertures.

Your assignment is to find an interesting foreground subject, get as close to it as your lens's minimum focusing distance allows, and shoot a series of five images, each focused on a different zone. Select an aperture of f/8, set ISO to 500, and test a 6-sec. exposure. Next, establish where the focal points are and where your eye is drawn and focus on these areas in your five images. Stack these images together in post-production to create a single frame with front-to-back sharpness.

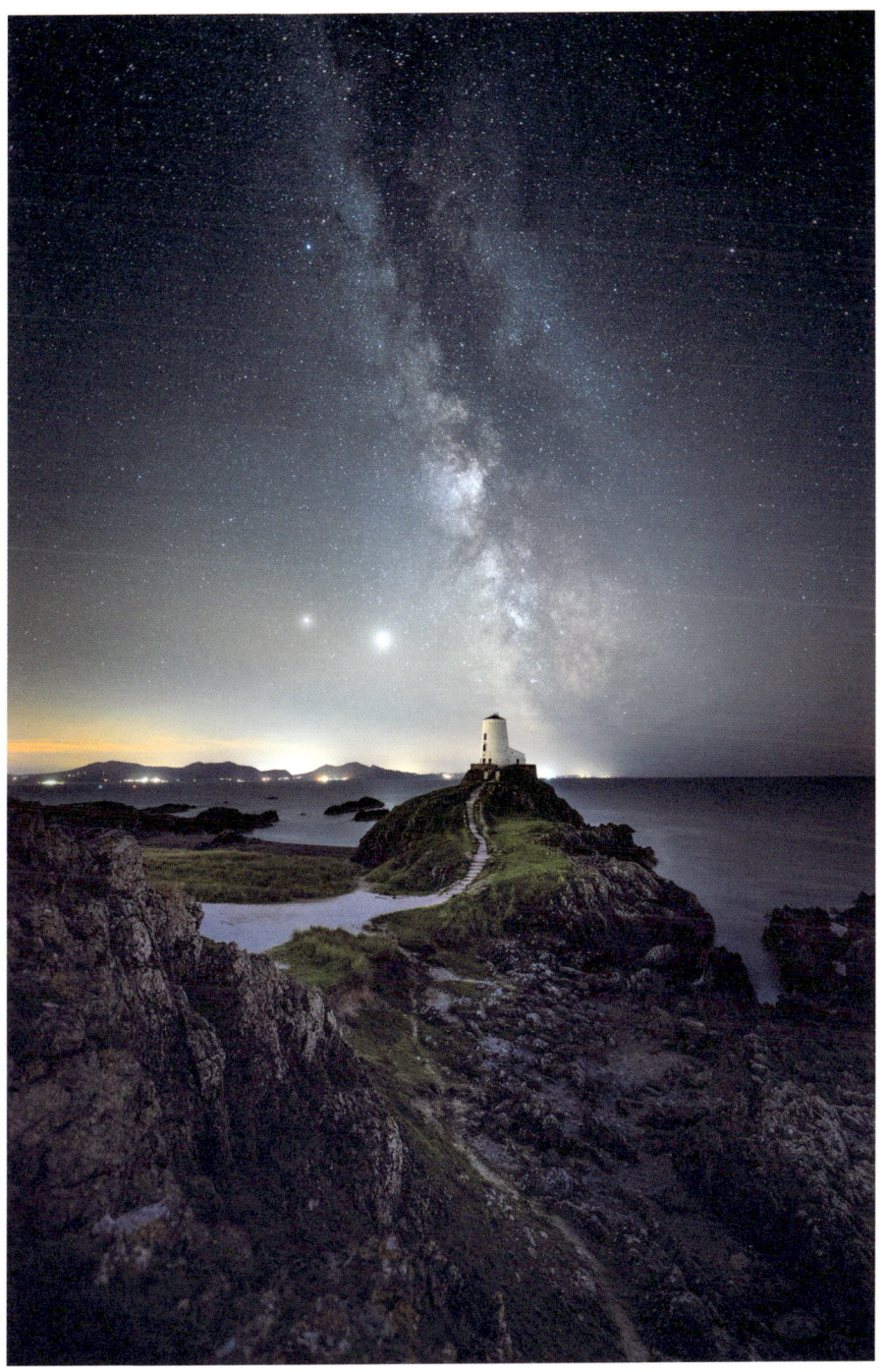

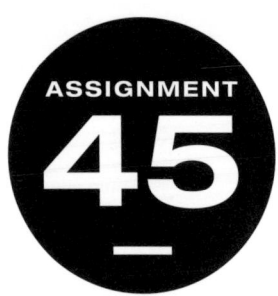

ASSIGNMENT
45

TIPS

- Use your post-processing software's lens correction tools to correct distortion.

- Be aware that prominent subjects placed toward the edges of the frame may become heavily distorted.

▶ *Using an ultra-wideangle lens allowed me to capture the breadth and immensity of the Milky Way shining over one of the moai statues of Easter Island.*

ULTRA-WIDE

Any lens with a focal length of 16mm or less is classed as an "ultra" wideangle lens. These specialist lenses are popular among night photographers, as their extreme field of view and strong visual distortion allow for a host of creative techniques.

Your assignment is to use an ultra-wideangle lens to shoot a starry landscape with a 180° field of view. The aim is to give the sky more coverage than your foreground subject. The image orientation can be influenced by your celestial subject, whether that be the Milky Way or a strong aurora forecast.

An ultra-wideangle lens's field of view is so vast that the effects of star trailing in exposures of up to 30 sec. will be less apparent, so prioritize a lower ISO setting over shutter speed for sharper, more defined images. To minimize distortion, avoid placing your foreground subject on the edge of the frame. In post-production, lens correction can be used to correct distortion in your images

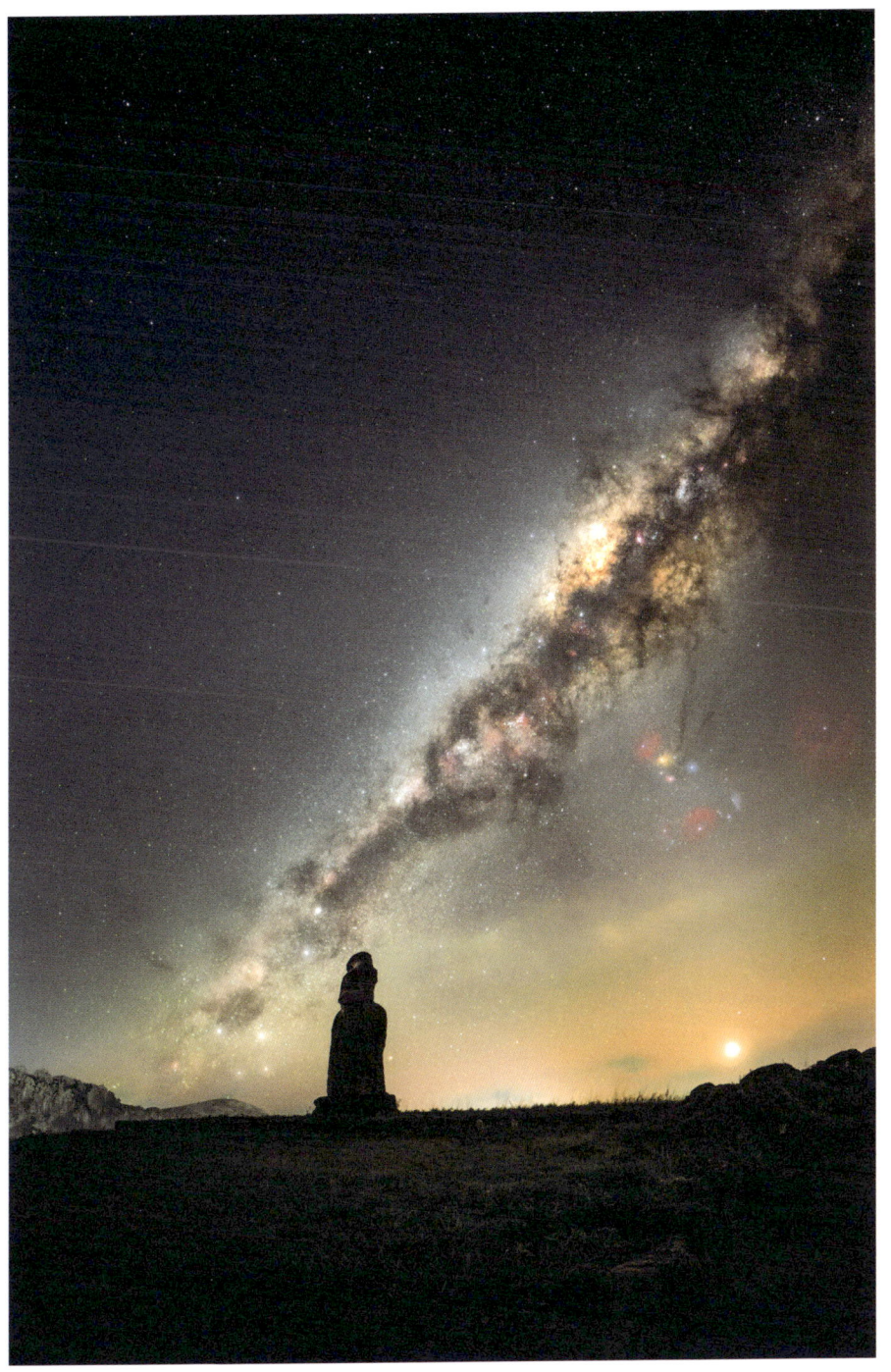

ASSIGNMENT

46

TIPS

- Your camera's white balance (WB) presets can be a good way to get started quickly. Choose an appropriate preset according to your location and light sources.

- Use the WB dropper in Lightroom to locate an area of neutral white balance. Select an area between the neutral-colored stars.

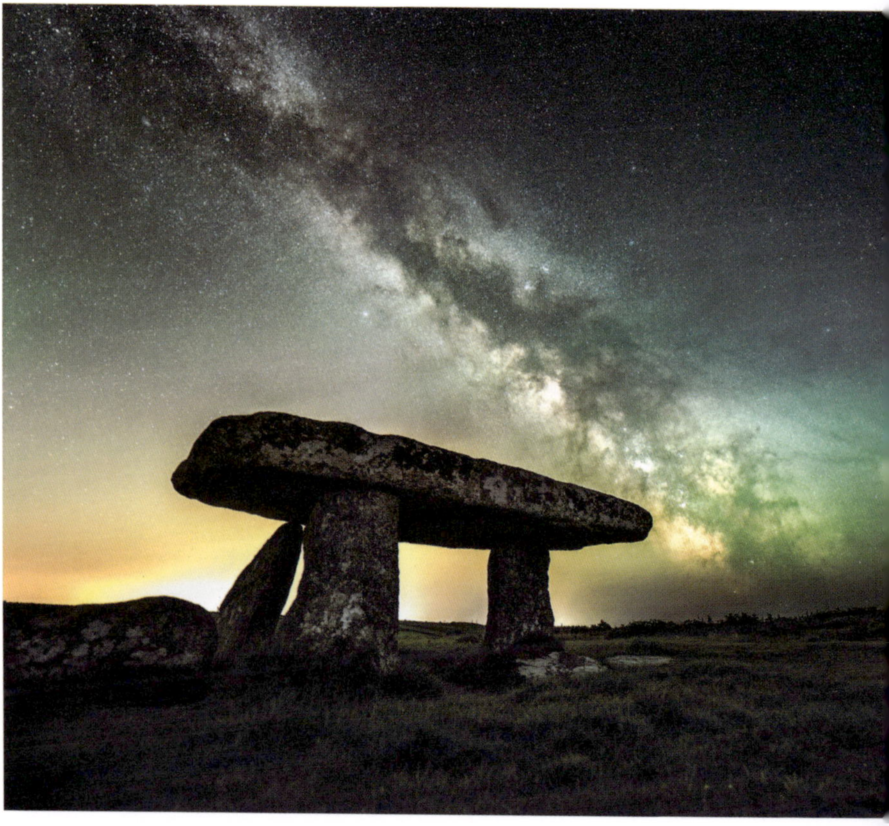

FINDING THE BALANCE

Whatever the subject, accurate white balance (WB) is the key to capturing images that are as close to nature as possible. But in night photography, it's even more important because of the need to preserve finer details. It's also more challenging due to changes in the weather, your location, light pollution, etc.

For this assignment, take a series of test shots of the night sky and find the WB setting that best suits your environment. Start with a WB of between 4,500 and 5,500 Kelvin (K), as this range gives a reliably accurate color temperature at night, being neither too warm nor too cold. Of course, this value will change according to your environment—sky glow from towns and cities will require warmer color temperatures for natural-looking images.

In post-processing software, start by pushing the Vibrance and Saturation adjustments all the way up to 100% to look at the color readout. Then use the Color

Temperature slider to achieve an image with a good mix of blue (cool) and orange (warm) hues. When you've found the sweet spot, reset the Vibrance and Saturation adjustments to their original settings and you will have achieved a perfectly neutral WB.

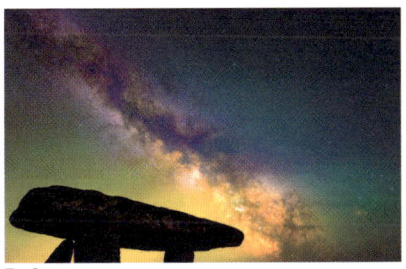

Before

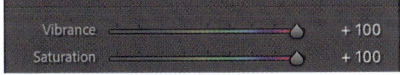

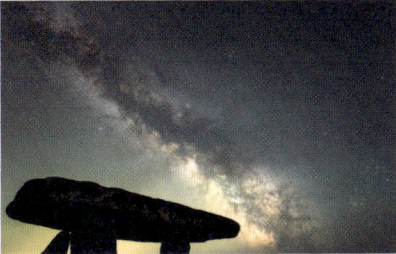

After

◄ *These before and after images show the importance of finding a good balance of blue and orange hues.*

ASSIGNMENT
47

TIPS

- Use layer masks and blending modes to merge exposures.

- If stacking your images to reduce noise, capture a single image of the stars to align your final composite with.

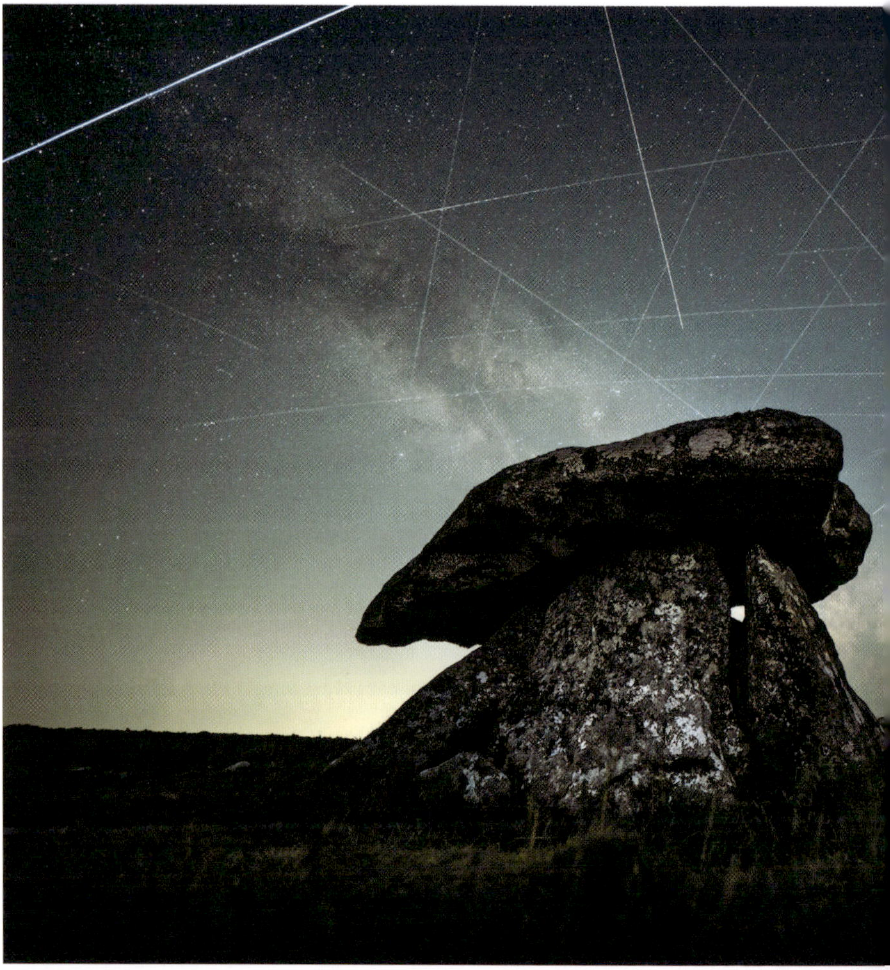

COMPOSITES

Composites that combine multiple images taken on different nights create a false sense of reality, which is why I strongly encourage you to always shoot your composite photos during the same night photography session, as this is the only way to capture true-to-nature images.

Composites allow photographers to solve problems. For instance, the example image here would have been impossible to capture in a single exposure due to number of satellites.

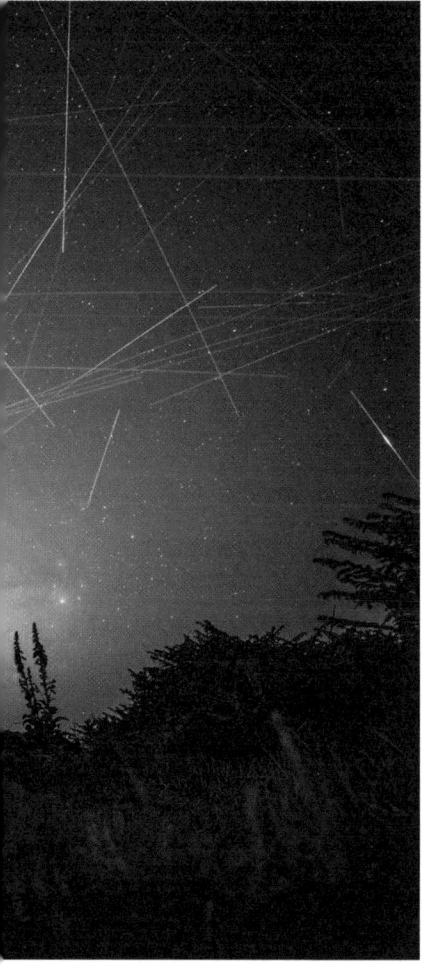

Your assignment is to create a composite of two or more frames of a similarly challenging scenario. Perhaps you need to balance the exposure of a light-polluted landscape or simply want to capture the apparent motion of a moonrise.

◀ *This composite image demontrates how pervasive satellites are in the sky above us, in a way that isn't possible in a single frame.*

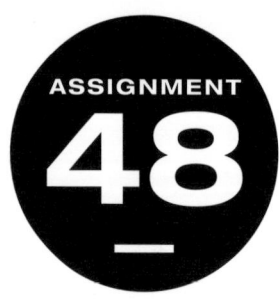

ASSIGNMENT
48
—

TIPS

- Inspiration can hit at any time. Make a note on your phone or have your journal to hand.

- When you come across a photo that strikes you as being truly original, take a moment to think about what makes it different. Is it the subject, the composition, the lighting, the camera's settings, or has the photographer simply broken the accepted rules?

KEEP A JOURNAL

It's difficult to be truly original in any artistic endeavor and night photography is no different. When dozens of night photographers stand in the same location and use the same lens to shoot the same subject, every image is going to look roughly the same. This is why I want you to spend some time thinking about what kind of subject matter truly excites you, then write your thoughts in a journal for future reference. There's often a fresh spin to apply to familiar subjects, but it sometimes takes a moment of inspiration to find it.

We will look at how to create unique images in bucket-list locations in Assignment 50, using different viewpoints, focal lengths, and camera orientations, but for this assignment we're going to get personal. What are you passionate about? What subjects and themes do you return to time and again? Where do you look for ideas?

Think about the books you read, the movies you watch, and the music you listen to. What themes stand out as interesting or unusual? By now, you should have gained the skills and confidence to shoot great night photographs. You should also have a good idea of which techniques appeal to you. So, grab a notebook and get scribbling, then put your newfound skills to the test. Originality starts here!

▶ *A self-portrait with the Glastonbury Festival's Pyramid Stage in the background and the Orion constellation above.*

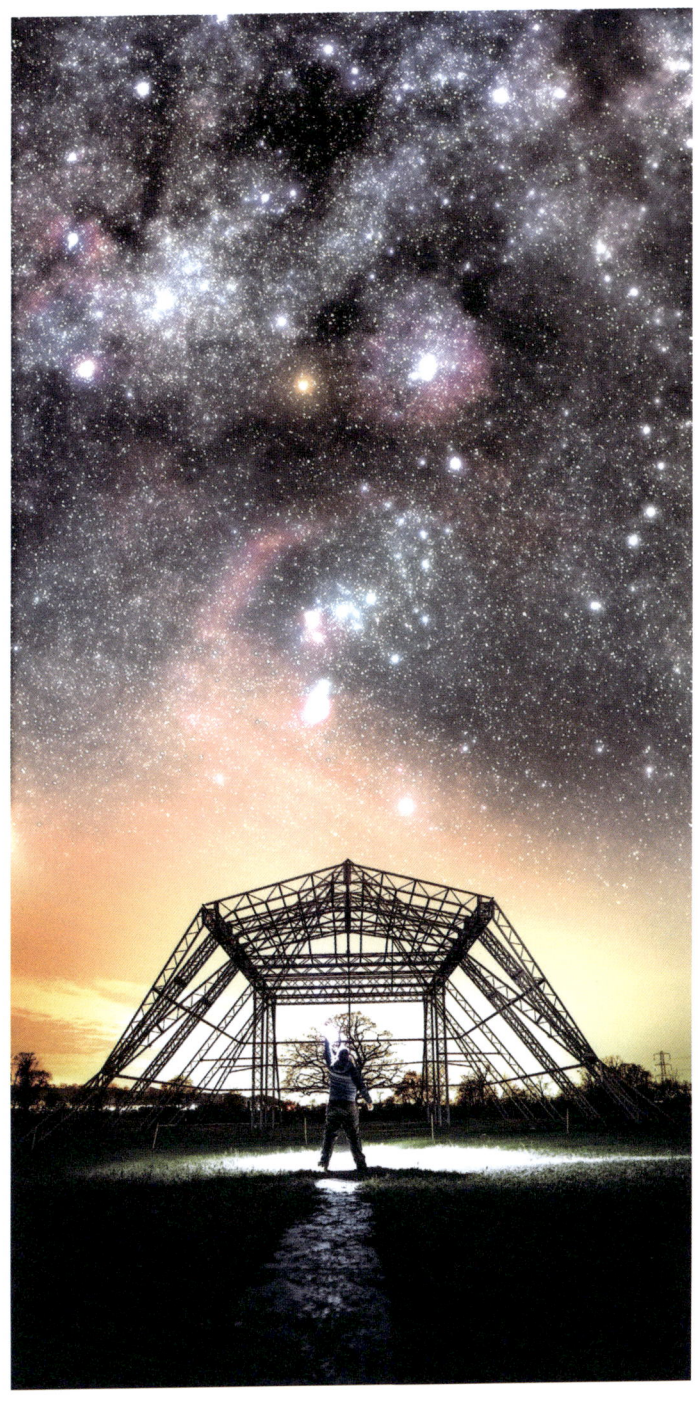

ASSIGNMENT 49

TIPS

- Carefully plan your compositions. For instance, if there are tall trees on one side of the frame, stand on the other side to ensure there are no branches in the frame. Alternatively, move your camera position.

- A head flashlight can add another dimension to your images, but be considerate if there are other photographers present, particularly if you're shooting in a dark-sky area, as the light from your flashlight could interfere with not only their exposures, but also the scene.

FIELD NOTES

If your foreground is very dark, you may need to illuminate the scene with a flashlight. Light "painting" allows you to brighten specific areas of the frame to capture more detail. However, you need to approach this technique with caution, as too much light will result in overexposure. Practice is key, so take a few test shots, using more or less light, until you are satisfied with the results.

► *This celestial self-portrait was taken in Tromsø, Norway—the northern lights capital of the world. The intensity of the aurora and clear weather forecast allowed for shorter exposures of around 4 sec. Unless you want to show movement, stay as still as possible.*

SELF-PORTRAITS

Nothing says "I was there!" quite like including yourself in a photograph of a once-in-a-lifetime event such as an eclipse or aurora. Not only does a nightscape self-portrait provide a great visual record of your experience, but it also lends a sense of scale to your subject. However, such images require some planning.

Perhaps the biggest challenge is focusing on the main subject—you. As you will be the focal point, it's important that you are pin-sharp, so you will need to pre-focus before you jump into the frame. A simple technique is to place a spare tripod or lens cap on the ground where you plan to stand and manually focus on this spot. You will also need a remote shutter release to time your shot and trigger the exposure—set it to take continuous images to increase your chances of capturing that one magic frame. Take a few test shots and review and refine the composition.

Once you are satisfied with your composition and exposure settings, it's time to experiment with different poses. Smile, leap into the air, stretch your arms out... there's no guarantee the celestial event you're photographing will happen again, so have fun and do your best to capture some memorable images. Just remember to stay in the area where you pre-focused to avoid any unwanted subject blur.

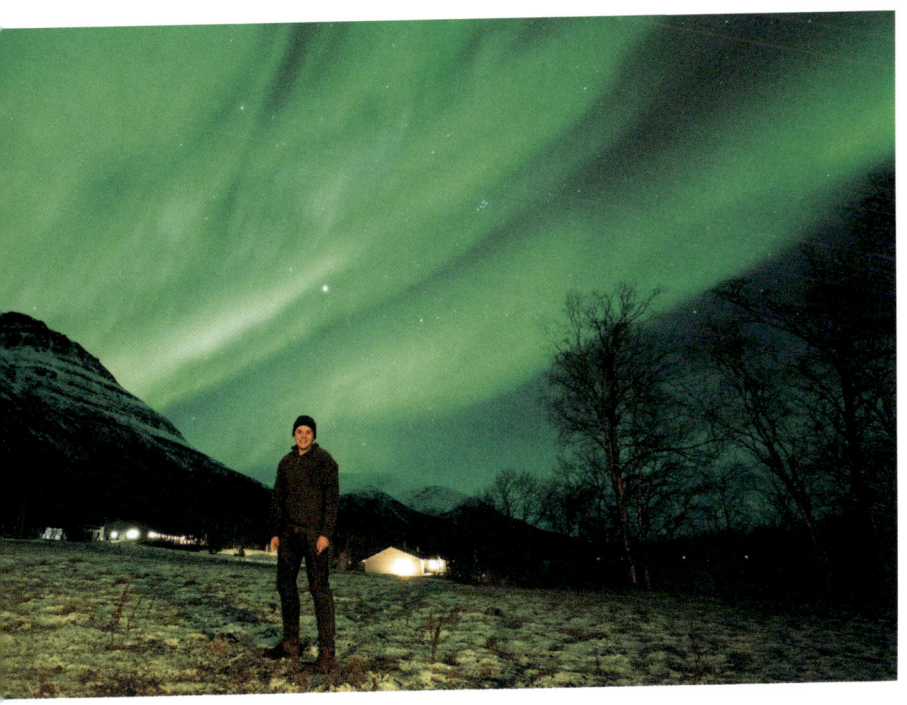

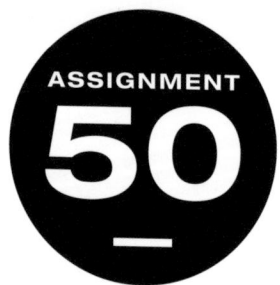

ASSIGNMENT 50

TIPS

- Other photographers will almost certainly be using flashlights during their exposures, so time your shots carefully to avoid any potential overexposure.

- Night photography at popular locations can be a lottery—some nights will be very busy, while others will be quiet. The only way to find out is to get out there and give it a go.

▶ *I needed to act quickly as the Milky Way began to rise above Durdle Door, and chose to shoot in portrait format to include as much of the night sky as possible.*

BUCKET-LIST LOCATIONS

Many aspiring night photographers will have a bucket list of popular locations to visit. From the Atacama Desert in Chile to La Palma in the Canary Islands, such beautiful places will take your breath away. But how do you create truly unique images of such well-photographed locations? And how do you focus on your craft when shooting alongside other photographers?

Your assignment is to create a unique photograph of a popular location. Once you've chosen your bucket-list hotspot, the first step is to recce it. Not only will this make for a fun day out, but it will also provide you with a list of potential viewpoints and compositions so you have plenty of back-up options should your first choice be too crowded. Next, use online and physical resources such as www.seasky.org and *Philip's Stargazing* to find out when a celestial event will take place or a feature of interest will be visible.

For my image of the Milky Way at Durdle Door, I decided to include wildflowers in my foreground to create a more unusual image of a location I've seen photographed thousands of times before. I could also have changed my camera's orientation, zoomed in or out, and opted for a higher or lower viewpoint. Take a range of images with different compositions and compare your results to the more typical images on social media. How successful were you in capturing a truly unique image?

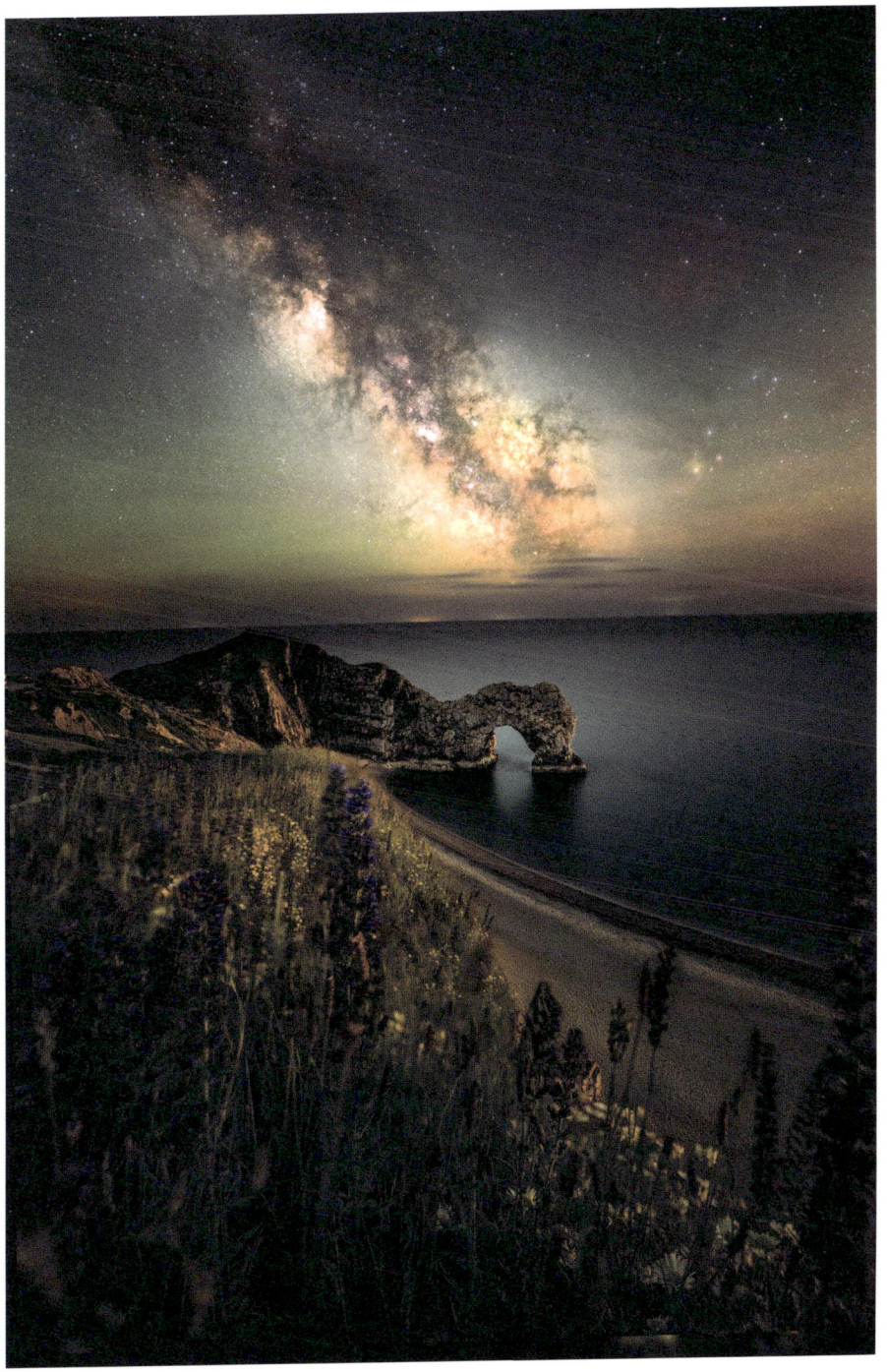

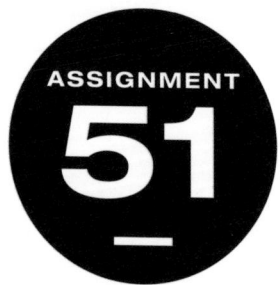

ASSIGNMENT 51

TIPS

- It's not always easy to predict clear skies, particularly when traveling overseas, so use long-range weather forecasts to increase your chances.

- If the weather isn't on your side, shoot longer exposures in which clouds can be utilized as another layer of visual interest.

▶ *Traveling across the world has allowed me to capture dynamic views of the universe, as was the case for the moai statues of Easter Island against a backdrop of the Milky Way.*

TRAVEL FURTHER AFIELD

As fulfilling as shooting local landscapes can be (see Assignment 35), there are some celestial subjects and events that cannot be photographed on your doorstep. Sometimes, night photography requires you to travel further afield and explore unchartered territories to see more of the natural wonders of the night sky.

Your challenge is to create a list of five images that could only be taken from further afield and sketch out your ideas and concepts. Research your destinations, whether in the same country or overseas, and use social media as a source of inspiration. Plan dates in conjunction with new moons so that skies are dark and use astronomy apps to find out which areas of the sky will be visible from a particular geographical location at a certain time of year.

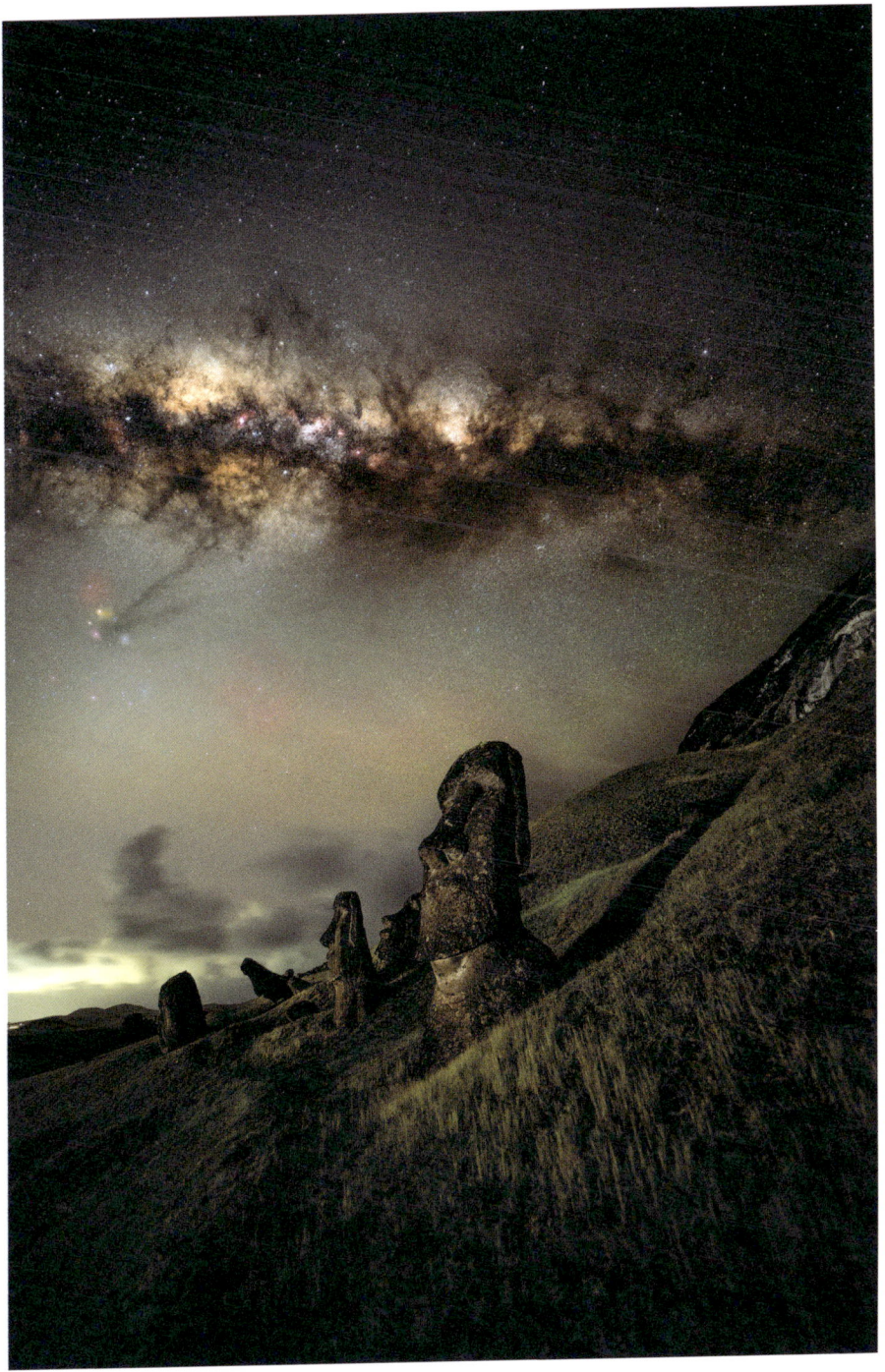

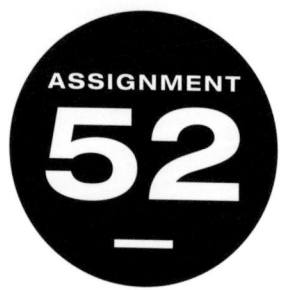

ASSIGNMENT
52

TIPS

- Never stop looking for inspiration and new ideas—every step you take will shape your style and creativity as a night photographer.

- Be open to new ideas and keep an eye out for what interesting techniques other photographers are using that you can adopt, such as fisheye images or narrowband imaging.

▶ *Never forget to have fun when taking your images. Here, I wave goodbye to a once-in-80,000-years comet, C/2023 A3 (Tsuchinshan–ATLAS).*

PERFECT YOUR ART

If you've been working through all the assignments in this book, you will now have greatly developed your knowledge of different photographic techniques and processes compared to when you first started on your journey.

For this final assignment, I'd like you to look at the shots you took for the earliest assignments in the book and pick out five that you feel you would approach differently had you had the knowledge and experience then that you now possess. Think about what you would change and then repeat the assignments—it may be that you'd choose a different subject, or you'd shoot at a different time of night, or with different settings. You may be happy with the subject and settings but want to bring in different camera or compositional techniques.

When you've taken and processed your new shots, compare them with the originals and reflect on not only how your artistic vision and creative process has evolved, but also on how it can continue to evolve in the future. Night photography is a matter of trial and error, so never stop exploring new and uncharted territories.

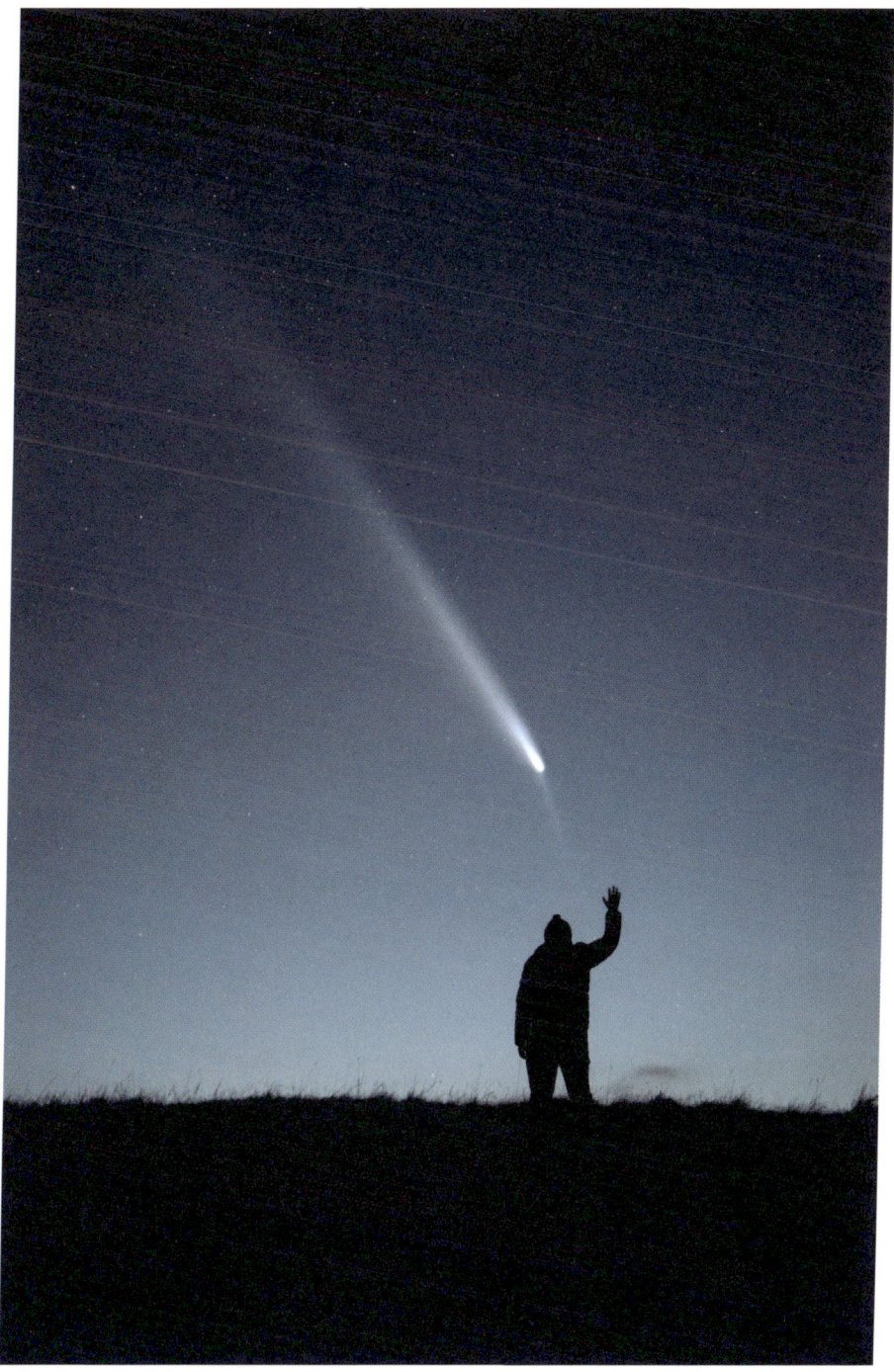

INDEX